Geographical Design

Spatial Cognition and Geographical Information Science

Second Edition

Synthesis Lectures on Human-Centered Informatics

Editor
John M. Carroll, *Penn State University*

Human-Centered Informatics (HCI) is the intersection of the cultural, the social, the cognitive, and the aesthetic with computing and information technology. It encompasses a huge range of issues, theories, technologies, designs, tools, environments, and human experiences in knowledge work, recreation and leisure activity, teaching and learning, and the potpourri of everyday life. The series publishes state-of-the-art syntheses, case studies, and tutorials in key areas. It shares the focus of leading international conferences in HCI.

Geographical Design: Spatial Cognition and Geographical Information Science
Second Edition
Stephen C. Hirtle

ISBN: 978-3-031-01098-9   paperback
ISBN: 978-3-031-00206-9   hard cover
ISBN: 978-3-031-02226-5   ebook

DOI 10.1007/978-3-031-02226-5

A Publication in the Springer series
SYNTHESIS LECTURES ON HUMAN-CENTERED INFORMATICS,
#43
Series Editor: John M. Carroll, Penn State University

Series ISSN: 1946-7680 Print   1946-7699 Electronic

Geographical Design

Spatial Cognition and Geographical Information Science

Second Edition

Stephen C. Hirtle
School of Information Sciences, University of Pittsburgh

SYNTHESIS LECTURES ON HUMAN-CENTERED INFORMATICS #43

ABSTRACT

With spatial technologies ranging from mapping software to the use of location-based services, spatial knowledge is often acquired and communicated through geographic information technologies. This book describes the interplay between spatial cognition research and use of spatial interfaces. It begins by reviewing what is known about how humans process spatial concepts and then moves on to discuss how interfaces can be improved to take advantage of those capabilities by disambiguating cognitive aspects, conceptual aspects, computational aspects, and communications aspects. Special attention is given to a variety of innovative geographical platforms that provide users with an intuitive understanding and support the further acquisition of spatial knowledge. Alternatives to shortest-path algorithms to explore more scenic routes, as well as individual user differences that can emerge from previous experiences with virtual spaces, are also discussed. The book concludes with a discussion of the number of outstanding issues, including the changing nature of maps as the primary spatial interface, concerns about privacy for spatial information, and looks at the future of user-centered spatial information systems.

KEYWORDS

cognitive maps, Geographic Information Science, GIScience, Geographic Information Systems, GIS, Global Positioning Systems, GPS, information visualization, landmarks, maps, navigation, privacy, regions, routes, social networks, spatial awareness, spatial cognition, user interfaces, volunteered geographic information, VGI

Contents

Figure Credits

Figure 2.1: National Research Council (2006). *Learning to think spatially*. Washington, DC: National Academies Press. DOI: 10.17226/11019.

Figure 2.3: Nothegger, C., Winter, S., and Raubal, M. (2004). Selection of salient features for route directions. *Spatial Cognition and Computation*, 4, pp. 113–136. Copyright © 2004, Taylor and Francis. Used with permission. DOI: 10.1207/s15427633scc0402_1.

Figure 3.6: Turner, A. (2009). The role of angularity in route choice. K. Hornsby, C. Claramunt, M. Denis and G. Ligozat, Eds. *Spatial Information Theory*, pp. 489–504. Springer Berlin/Heidelberg. Copyright © 2009, Springer. Used with permission.

Figure 3.8: Skupin, A. and Fabrikant, S. (2008). Spatialization. J. Wilson and S. Fotheringham, Eds. *The Handbook of Geographical Information Science*. Blackwell Publishing. Copyright © 2008, Wiley, pp. 61–79. Used with permission.

Figure 4.3: Lee, J., Forlizzi, J., and Hudson, S. (2008). Iterative design of MOVE: A situationally appropriate vehicle navigation system. *International Journal of Human-Computer Studies*, 66(3), 198–215. Copyright © 2008 Elsevier. Used with permission.

Figure 4.5: Priedhorsky, R., Jordan, B., and Terveen, L. (2007). How a personalized geowiki can help bicyclists share information more effectively. *Proceedings of the 2007 International Symposium on Wikis*, Montreal, Quebec, Canada: ACM. Copyright © 2007, ACM, pp. 93–98. Used with permission. DOI: 10.1145/1296951.1296962.

Acknowledgments

The ideas presented in this book were developed through conversations and interactions with a number of colleagues and co-authors. I particularly want to thank Max Egenhofer, Andrew Frank, Christian Freksa, Tommy Gärling, Michael Goodchild, Werner Kuhn, David Mark, Dan Montello, Kai Olsen, Juval Portugali, Sabine Timpf, and Albert Yeap, who have supported extended visits and sabbatical opportunities over the past 20 years.

I also appreciate many discussions over the years about geographical and spatial issues that I have had with Gary Allen, Guoray Cai, Tony Cohen, Clare Davies, Matt Duckham, Patrick Dudas, Bob Firth, Alex Klippel, Prashant Krisnamurthy, Brian Heidorn, John Jonides, Alan MacEachren, Tim McNamara, Paul Munro, Kai-Florian Richter, Cristina Robles Bahm, Barry Smith, Molly Sorrows, Samvith Srinivas, Thora Tenbrink, Barbara Tversky, Stephen Winter, and Mike Worboys. My understanding of the critical issues has been influenced by their insights and critiques.

Finally, I wish to thank Colin Ellard, Sara Fabrikant, and Scott Freundschuh, for their detailed comments on an earlier draft of the manuscript, with the understanding that any remaining mistakes and confusions remain my sole responsibility.

CHAPTER 1

Introduction

We live in a world where spatial information is becoming ubiquitous as mobile phones, navigation systems, mapping services and other geographical tools are now commonplace and often part of the tools we use every day. Such services have dramatically changed the way in which individuals acquire, use, transmit, and generally interact with spatial information. Even a modest digital camera can automatically record the time and spatial location that a photograph was taken. Not only does this remove any need for personal note-taking of these details, which only the most dedicated photographer would have done so in the past, but it is now possible for others to follow the timeline that the photographer took in recording a set of vacation photographs (Popescu and Grefenstette, 2009). More common is how many of us now carry devices in our pockets that will let us know how far it is to the nearest gas station, what is around us in terms of restaurants, shopping, or even our friends, as well as access to all the information on the world wide web.

Unfortunately, this new world is not all rosy. I am reminded of a recent story that was recounted to me by friend. Her teenage son had been driving himself to the hockey practice for about a month, when her car had to go into the shop for repair. When she said that he would have to take his dad's car, the son balked and said that he can't as there was no Global Positioning Systems (GPS) and he didn't know the way. The mother reminded him that he had been driving for month to the hockey rink, to which her son responded "I don't pay attention when I am driving. I just follow the GPS." While anecdotal, there is solid research that supports the idea that spatial information is not automatically encoded during guided trips to be used in future, unguided trips (Ellard, 2009; Parush, Ahuvia, and Erev, 2007). Thus, the enigma of this new world is that while spatial information is readily available, spatial knowledge, and spatial skills are lagging. Simply put, our GPS knows where the restaurant is located, so why should we bother learning it, as well.

In this light, this book will review the interplay between spatial cognition research and the use of spatial interfaces. In particular, the focus will center on what is known about how humans process spatial concepts and how interfaces can be improved to take advantage to that understanding. After reviewing the cognitive literature, there is a brief discussion of available geographical technologies. This is followed by a look at approaches and technologies that support *spatial awareness* in addition to *spatial assistance*. The book should prove useful to those who want to include spatial information in interface design in ways that reflect the cognitive constraints that we all carry with us.

Spatial interfaces discussed in this book are taken in the broad sense to include reference maps, quantitative (statistical) maps, qualitative (thematic) maps, route maps, navigational charts, mobile maps, as well as spatial displays of non-geographic data. The approach builds on a long and valuable history in the field of cartography that informs much of the theory. At the same time, the growth of digital mapping, in both desktop and mobile settings, has resulted in a new set of norms, which have replaced paper maps with fluid displays that are zoomable, multilayered and easily can change perspective or content. In the electronic world, many standard cartographic principles, such as selecting the appropriate scale, turn out to be less relevant, while other design choices, such as the fluidity of zooming, become more important. In addition, the interplay between data mining and graphical presentation is leading to new advances in graphical methods that will continue to evolve (Andrienko and Andrienko, 1999, 2006). At the same time, the need to understand spatial processing and spatial cognition, which is the focus of this book, will be important regardless of the nature of the graphical display and geographic design.

CHAPTER 2

Spatial Cognition

While empirical research in spatial cognition dates back to Trowbridge (1913) and Tolman (1948), the era of modern research is about 30 years old when a large number of papers started to appear that specifically focused on the mental representations of spatial knowledge (e.g., Evans and Pezdek, 1980; Holyoak and Mah, 1982; Stevens and Coupe, 1978; Thorndyke and Hayes-Roth, 1982; Tversky, 1981). In concert with one of the first papers in this time period that showed systematic distortions in spatial memory (Stevens and Coupe, 1978), researchers have continued to document numerous ways in which physical and mental space differ. Together, this line of research has suggested that spatial knowledge is not veridical with physical space, but is distorted by categorical membership, boundaries, and dominant spatial axes (Kitchin and Blades, 2002; Mark et al., 1999; Montello and Freundschuh, 2005; Tversky, 2000). More recently, Newcombe (2018) has stressed that the term "spatial cognition" itself is multi-faceted with at least three kinds of functions: navigation (as used for moving through space), tool use and invention (as a seamstress or sculptor might engage in), and spatialization (as used in abstract spatial reasoning). Here, the focus will be on the first use of the term that includes memory for location, route planning, and spatial organization with a focus on the perception of space, in addition, to the location and extent of the actual physical space.

The notion that perceived space differs from actual space, led Egenhofer and Mark (1995) to posit the existence of *a Naïve Geography* that individuals have about the geographic world. Naïve Geography is not unlike the Naïve Physics, which was an approach that was useful in building inference engines in the early days of AI (Hayes, 1979, 1989). Naïve Geography represents a common-sense view of the world, complete with misconceptions and biases. As such, it can form a basis for how the next generation of geographic information systems should respond to a user's needs. According to Egenhofer and Mark (1995), the elements of Naïve Geography included observations such as (1) geographic space is two-dimensional, (2) the Earth is perceived as flat, (3) maps are more real that experience, (4) geographic entities are ontologically different from enlarged table-top objects, (5) space and time are tightly coupled, (6) geographic information is frequently incomplete, (7) people use multiple conceptions of space, (8) space has multiple levels of detail, (9) boundaries are sometimes entities, sometimes not, (10) topology matters, metric refines, (11) people have biases toward the compass axes, and (12) distances are asymmetric and do not easily add up.

Each of these observations has implications for how space is accessed and processed by humans. For example, the idea that space and time are tightly coupled (property 5), means that if asked how far it is to a location, it is not at all unusual to describe a place as two hours away rather than in terms of linear measurements (Hirtle and Mascolo, 1991). In terms of the multiple conceptions of space (property 7), one can think of cities as both points (it is 185 km from Pittsburgh to Cleveland) and areas (Pittsburgh covers 151 sq km). Egenhofer and Mark (1995) argued that spatial queries should be able to handle such conceptualizations without mixing the two unnecessarily.

The reality of many modern spatial information systems is that spatial queries are taken literally. An earlier search of bus system routes in Pittsburgh,[1] with the option of "has the least amount of walking," generated a trip that would take 157 minutes on three different buses, including a 61-minute wait for the second transfer. In contrast, the direct bus took only 22 minutes, leaving from the same start location, and arriving only just one block away from the final location. The direct bus resulted in a slight increase in the amount of walking, which caused it to be rejected. Unfortunately, this kind of spatial-temporal tradeoff, which humans would do easily, remains a challenge for some simplistic information systems.

Another principle of Naïve Geography is the notion that the world is perceived as flat (property 2). This principle leads to common misunderstandings that are hard to correct. For example, many airline passengers are confused as to why flights between the U.S. and Europe fly over Greenland or Iceland, when those locations appear to be so far north on the flat maps shown in the back of airline magazines. Even the *Economist*, in 2003, printed and then retracted a visualization of the North Korean threat of missile attacks, which initially plotted circles on a Mercator projection of the Earth, shown in Figure 2.1(a). Of course, the true reach of the missiles would be equidistant on the globe, which when then drawn on the Mercator projection results in a different level of threat, as shown in Figure 2.1(b). A report by National Academy entitled *Learning to Think Spatially: GIS as a Support System in the K-12 Curriculum* (Downs, 2006) documented this all but too common example as why spatial thinking needs to be taught explicitly in schools. Spatial thinking does not come easy or naturally, and the common occurrence of seeing world drawn on a flat map can lead to a great misunderstanding of spatial relationships. At the same time, spatial thinking has not yet reached the level of reading or mathematical skills in the U.S. educational system, which adds to the problem.

While Naïve Geography is a theoretical framework with many untested assumptions, there is related research that is well grounded in empirical studies. The following sections discuss several specific principles of spatial cognition that are particularly relevant to the building of human-computer interfaces and web-based systems that implicitly or explicitly include spatial information. By accounting for these principles, it is possible to build information systems that will augment spatial knowledge, while providing spatial information in an easy to grasp and intuitive manner (Haklay, 2010).

---

[1] http://www.portauthority.org/

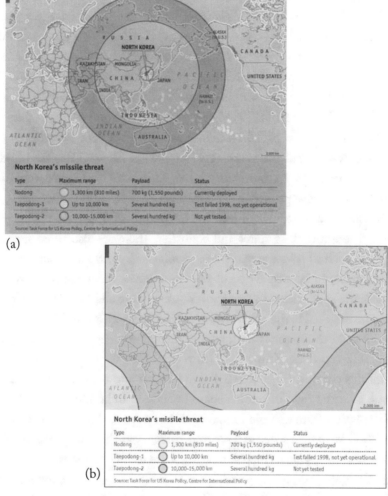

Figure 2.1: Example from the *Economist* from 2003 which (a) erroneously indicated two missile ranges by concentric circles on a Mercator projection. The correct map (b) was published two weeks later (Downs, 2006)

2.1   CONCEPTUALIZATION OF SPACE

As a first principle, it is important to understand how geographical knowledge is characterized by its scale of coverage. Memory for spaces have been studied formally by psychologists, geographers and others, since the early 1900s. However, psychologists have typically studied small spaces, such as rooms or even table-tops, while geographers are more likely to study memories for towns and cities. Freundshuh and Egenhofer (1997), among others, argued that this distinction is important, as human spatial cognition seems to operate differently in small scale spaces than in large scale spaces. In the Naïve Geography conceptualization, it was stated that (4) "geographic entities are ontologically different from enlarged table-top objects." However, a geographical information system (GIS) enables us to interact with large scale spaces as if they were small scale (Frank, 1996) and therefore this mismatch can lead to confusions (Freundschuh and Egenhofer, 1997). Thus, it is critical to understand the type of space that one is modeling with a spatial information system.

Freundschuh and Egenhofer (1997) review 15 different ontological parsings of the physical world, then propose unified view based on manipulability of objects, locomotion of the observer and size of the space. A subset of their summary is shown in Figure 2.2 with the addition of their own new conceptualization. In Freundschuh and Egenhofer's (1997) conceptualization, the two primary categories that involve geographical information are *environmental spaces*, which refer to neighborhood size spaces that require movement to comprehend, and *geographic spaces*, which are too large to move through such as states and countries. There are also three special cases of *manipulable object spaces*, such as *table-top spaces*, *non-manipulable object spaces*, such as one's immediate living and working space, and a special case of *panoramic spaces*, which are very large spaces that can be viewed from a single spot, such as a scenic overlook or large auditorium. Finally, there is a sixth category that runs orthogonal to the other five, which are the *map spaces*. Map spaces are interesting in that they can be used to represent both environmental and geographic spaces, but they are in some ways like a table-top space. Kuipers (1978) was perhaps the most ardent in arguing that our memory which locates continental U.S. in between Canada and Mexico is not unlike our memory that our telephone is to the right of our keyboard on a desk. In both cases, one learns spatial relations through observation from a single vantage point of a spatial layout. In contrast, Freundschuh and Egenhofer (1997) keep map space as a separate category as there are a variety of symbolic (map symbols) and hierarchical relations (map scaling) that are unique to maps.

Maps are also unique in often creating an orientation specific representation (Evans and Pezdek, 1980; Sholl and Nolin, 1997). That is, spaces learned only by maps, such as in world geography, are learned with a single, preferred orientation. This helps explain why a world map that puts the south pole at the top would be viewed as "upside-down" (MacEachren, 1995), but a shopping mall directory that not aligned with your visual orientation, regardless of south, is confusing (Klippel, Hirtle, and Davies, 2010; Levine, 1982). Thus, the distinctions made by Freundschuh and Egenhofer (1997) are important when for considering what kinds of representations and what kinds of operations on those representations might be useful given a specific geographical scale.

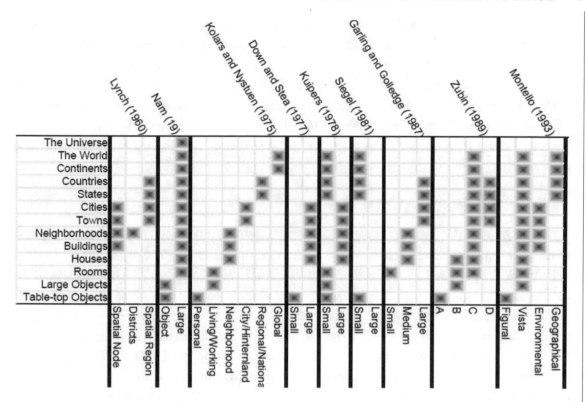

Figure 2.2: Models of space as a function of size.

Recent research has looked at the ability to gain knowledge from reading maps to demonstrate that it is a function of both the map display and ability of the reader to draw proper conclusions based on that display. Ishikawa (2016) conducted an in-depth study of graduate students in various disciplines, such as economics, literature, computer science and geography, who were taking an introductory GIScience class. He found that in contrast to the low-spatial students, high-spatial students organized concepts in a way that was similar to experts in the field. Furthermore, the high-spatial students would objectively compare multiple sources of information to answer the spatial questions. That is, high-spatial students' geospatial conceptions match experts' conceptions to a greater degree than those of low-spatial students (Ishikawa, 2016).

One can also gain insight into the conceptualization of space by the modeling of spatial knowledge in the field of robotics. Rather than assuming that robots gain global knowledge by integrating successive views to form a global map, Yeap and Hossain (2019) argue that cognitive mapping begins by computing, in increasing order of complexity, a point map, a local map, a route map, and a series of disjointed global maps. Their model provides a formal model without the need for a single unified global map. Extending this to human wayfinding, it would account for the episodes where one taking an unfamiliar route suddenly finds themselves close to their goal, indicating a lack of a consistent, global map, which would not have generated the sense of surprise.

The evolution of cognitive maps can also be altered by a change in barriers that divide local spaces. Szekely and Kotosz (2018) found an asymmetry in views along the Serbian-Hungarian border, where some residents saw the division as simply a border crossing, others envisioned to be fence or a wall. Furthermore, from 2003–2016 there was increase among residents to represent the boundary as a physical boundary as a result of political dialogs as presented by through the local news reports.

2.1.1   FUNDAMENTAL CONCEPTS

Before addressing the details of research on spatial cognition, it is helpful to introduce the fundamental concepts that have been addressed in the scientific literature. In a recent review, Liu and Schunn (2017) proposed a list of central questions that have been addressed by researchers in the field of spatial cognition regarding spatial representations in terms organization, form, and development. For example, functional models of space differentiate between the space of the body, the space around the body, the space of navigation and the space of external representations (Tverksy, 2003). The focus here is on the third level: the space of navigation, in which the mental map of the space must be integrated from many partial bits of knowledge that use separate and distinct reference frames. In addition to functional models, Liu and Schunn (2017) review neuropsychological models of space and computational models of space, followed by an examination of how spatial skills are acquired.

In related work, Duckham (2015) identified the minimal set of expert topics that are shared by researchers in the field of geographical information science (GIScience), which address the conceptualizations, as opposed to the techniques, use by those interested in space and geography. In particular, he examined the extent to which recent papers focused on (1) the underlying structure of geographic information, (2) the uncertainty and/or vagueness of spatial information, (3) the dynamics of spatial information, (4) the language and cognition of space, and (5) cartographic design. The work both highlights areas of shared expertise among a diverse set of researchers and benefit of interdisciplinary collaborations.

2.1.2   DIMENSIONALITY

While much of the research on navigation treats space has being two-dimensional, there are many situations where considering variation in height to be important, in contrast to the two-dimensional displays shown by maps and most in-car navigation systems. Unfortunately, few navigation systems take advantage of this concept by instructing users to "go up the hill" or "take the road down into the valley," as one would often find in human-generated directions be they written or oral. Even in the abstract domain of document space, Chalmers (1993) calls our everyday world to be 2.1 dimensional, with some academic fields producing "piles" of documents on a given topic, while other areas somewhat "sparse" in terms of publications.

Recent studies exploring dimensionality and neural encoding have begun to document some interesting effects, which contradict a simple two-dimensional view of the world. For example, Kim and Maguire (2018) found that the performance of participants, who had to remember the location of objects in a two-story, eight-room building, demonstrated that the vertical and the horizontal location information was similarly encoded in terms of both the behavioral and neural findings, thus suggesting that full three-dimensional encodings of spatial locations are possible.

2.2   COGNITIVE STRUCTURES

The second distinction that will prove important is the recognition of various cognitive structures that are imposed on geographic space. In one of the earliest and most influential works, Lynch (1960) argued that the structure of the city consisted of paths, edges, districts, nodes, and landmarks. One can think of these structures in terms of dimensions. *Nodes*, which are locations where paths converge, and *landmarks*, which are visually prominent locations, can be thought of as zero-dimensional objects. One-dimensional objects are the *paths*, which are the familiar routes that are used to move around the city, and *edges*, which separate districts. Finally, *districts* are two-dimensional areas that have a common identifying character, such as neighborhood or central shopping district.

Several of Lynch's elements have been refined over the years by additional empirical work in the cognitive science literature. Hirtle and Jonides (1985) demonstrated how clustering methods can determine neighborhood membership by individual. Furthermore, judgments of distance are systematically distorted with between-cluster judgments of distance consistently longer than within-cluster judgments. McNamara, Hardy, and Hirtle (1989) showed similar effects with learned locations on both a paper map and objects in a room. Similar effects with fixed boundaries have been shown by many others (e.g., Friedman and Brown, 2000; Friedman and Montello, 2006) More recently, Uttal et al. (2010) have shown that biases due to categorical information becomes more biased with time. In their case, they looked at judgments between the north and south parts of the Northwestern campus, which have no clear division. Uttal et al. were led to study the division when he overhead students from the South campus area making comments like "This better be good, because I don't go to North Campus for nothing," even though the walk was only six-minute from their dorm. [2]

The Lynchian elements were also seen as relevant to the spatial representations that taxi drivers have cities in an early study by Chase (1983). In particular, the hierarchical organization of neighborhoods was important in terms of the economy of storage and, at the same time, was an

---

[2] http://www.northwestern.edu/newscenter/stories/2011/01/spatial-memory.html

integral part of planning routes. Chang et al. (2006) has used the hierarchical structure of the city to reduce the number of polygons needed to create legible visualizations of complex urban environments. Recent work by Dias and Ramadier (2015) suggests an interesting relationship between social and cognitive structure in which they reported that spatial representations depend on the social trajectory of individuals (which can be upward, downward, or stable compared to the social status of the parents).

2.2.1   LANDMARKS

In addition to regions, the notion of landmarks has achieved much attention in the literature, in part due to the importance of landmarks for navigation. Sorrows and Hirtle (1999) developed a formal theory of landmarks for both geographical spaces and information spaces. "Landmarkedness" was seen to be quality that could be measured in different ways.

- *Visual landmarks* were visually distinctive, like Lynch's landmarks.

- *Structural landmarks* are important nodes of intersecting paths, regardless if they were visually distinctive or not.

- *Semantic,* or *cognitive, landmarks* have a unique meaning that stands out, such as the central information center in most European cities.

To examine how the theory of landmarks could be used to identify potential landmarks, Nothegger, Winter, and Raubal (2004) ran a small test study using a route in the center of Vienna. The route was pre-chosen, but the question at hand was how to describe the route to a pedestrian using landmarks. For example, one could ask which building at Intersection 7 in Figure 2.3 should be chosen to when stating "Turn right at the _____ building." The photograph shows the eight possible buildings at the intersection. Each building was coded in terms of visual and semantic salience. Structural salience was not measured in this study since the route was predetermined and all locations would share the same structural salience. (In another scenario, one might use salience to pick the best route, but that was not done in this case.)

Nothegger, Winter, and Raubal (2004) measured visual salience by measuring the façade size, the façade shape as deviation from square, façade color in terms of average RGB and HSB, and the façade visibility as measured in terms of line of site. Semantic salience was measured in terms of the cultural importance and identifiability of the building. Total salience was calculated as a weighted average of the individual scores, with Building No. 5 with its unique architecture and significance having the high salience score (12.4). As confirmation of the salience rating, it was found that 26 of 40 subjects also chose this location as the most salient among the eight alternatives. Further research described in Section 4.2 has suggested how yellow pages and other commercial directories might be used to find landmarks to use in directions automatically (Duckham, Winter, and Robinson, 2010). In more recent work, Bartie et al. (2014) highlighted some of the conceptual problems that must be overcome to implement this kind of algorithm. For example, in finding landmarks in Edinburgh, Scotland, the same building might be denoted as a *church*, a *church spire*, a *church tower*, a *clock tower*, or the *town clock*. In all cases, it is visually distinct and spatially located in the same spot, but the identify tag by residents could vary greatly.

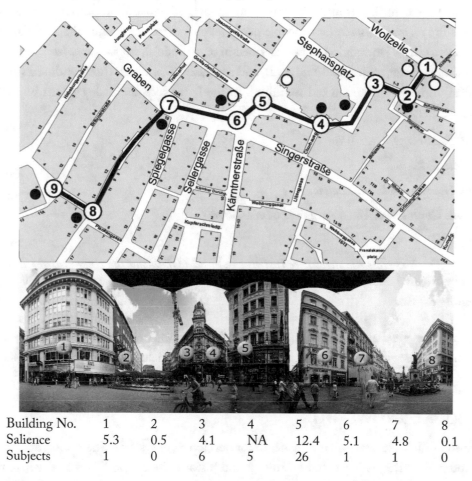

Building No.	1	2	3	4	5	6	7	8
Salience	5.3	0.5	4.1	NA	12.4	5.1	4.8	0.1
Subjects	1	0	6	5	26	1	1	0

Note: Salience indicates rating for each building at Intersection 7. Subjects indicates the number of subjects who independently chose that building as the most salient for the intersection.

Figure 2.3: Choosing most salient landmarks at a route turn in Vienna (Nothegger et al., 2004).

One approach to defining landmarks, which previously required local knowledge, as given by Zhu and Karimi (2014). Their paper demonstrated a technique based on a neural network model, where both static and dynamic features are used for selecting landmarks automatically.

Experiments on the technique showed that rule-based labeling based on visual characteristics had a precision of approximately 90%, which makes the technique suitable and reliable for automatic selection of landmarks.

The nature of landmarks was the sole topic of recent book by Richter and Winter (2014), which argued the importance of landmarks for spatial cognition, while documenting the variety of roles that they can play, from their visual, functional, or semantic importance. In their book, they discuss the *cognitive aspects* (how people perceive, memorize, think and talk about landmarks), *conceptual aspects* (how landmarks can be described in data models), *computational aspects* (how landmarks can be observed, stored, and analyzed), and *communication aspects* (how landmarks enrich the communication between human and machine). In the latter case, the dialog might be envisioned for a start as follows:

> *You: Excuse me?*
>
> *Guide: Yes?*
>
> *You: How do I get to Chinatown?*
>
> *Guide: Chinatown? You mean Little Bourke Street?*
>
> *You: Yes.*
>
> *Guide: Ok. You cross the street here (points east) and walk along the river past the casino. Then you cross another big street—Queens Bridge. Just behind that street there is a footbridge crossing the river…*

In this case, the dialog is suggestive of steps often involved in human-to-human communication that one might wish to encode for a human-to-machine dialog. The differences between these two modes of communication will be discussed further in Chapter 4.

2.2.2   LOCAL KNOWLEDGE

The inclusion of local knowledge is of concern for developers of systems. The notion of what makes a good landmark varies widely based on culture and history. The classic "Turn Left where the Old Barn use to be," may sound funny, but is not uncommon. Sports arena, for example, often have nicknames that you might not find in an atlas. In Pittsburgh, any local taxi cab driver would know where the "The Igloo", known formerly as the "Civic Arena" and home to Pittsburgh Penguins NHL team, was located, despite not being listed in any formal database of locations under that name.

In related work, Chen, Vasardani, and Winter (2017) developed a method to disambiguate fine-grained place names from everyday place descriptions through the use of cluster analysis. This problem might be explained by this imaginary scenario from Kim, Vasardani and Winter (2017) of an emergency call from a college campus.

Emergency call scenario. – This is the triple zero service, what is your emergency?

Hello. . .! I am calling from the University of Melbourne. There has been an accident and a student is in dire straits. We need an ambulance. We are in the Cussonia Courtyard, in the middle of the campus. The Courtyard is next to the clock-tower.

Which street is the nearest to your location?

I cannot say from the top of my head, but I think Monash Road is closest to the courtyard. Coming from Monash Road, you can rush through the Old Quad. The courtyard is just behind the Old Quad.

In a tragic way, this kind of dialog points out the difference between the service provider that is expecting exact road names and building numbers and the service requester that can only provide visual cues. One might add that there may be a simple technological solution of simply relaying the global coordinates of where the emergency call has is coming from if such information is not being blocked for privacy concerns and that the call is be generated from the location that the assistance is needed.

2.2.3   COGNITIVE COLLAGE

While term *cognitive map* (Tolman, 1948) has been used by many to refer to the underlying representation of spatial entities, it can unfortunately cause one to regard the representational properties as strictly "map-like." In contrast, the mental representation appears to be much more disparate and complex. Tversky (1993) used the metaphor of a *cognitive collage* to better describe the nature of spatial knowledge. In this regard, the mental representation of spatial objects is a fragmented collection of partially overlapping bits of knowledge, where individual bits might be spatial, visual or textual. A cognitive collage, as envisioned by Tversky, is related to other conceptualizations, such as cognitive atlas (Hirtle, 1998; Kuipers, 1982) or inter-representation networks (Portugali, 1996). The cognitive collage asserts that geographic information can consist of spatial, visual, and verbal information. The spatial components are not veridical in the sense of matching the Earth, but might be twisted and deformed. Lynch (1960) called this a rubber sheet model, as if the map was pulled and distorted like a piece of rubber, but not folded like a napkin. The rubber sheet is probably too strong in that you might have disparate pieces in your mind. Thinking of Miami as due south of New York (which it is not) would be tugging on the rubber sheet model of the U.S. On the other hand, realizing the Great Britain is separated from Belgian by the English Channel, while not being sure of the direction from London to Brussells, would be more in line with the collage, as the pieces are coherent, but the relationship between them is somewhat vague.

More importantly for our discussion, the cognitive collage will also have images, sounds, numerical information, facts, and text. Thus, one might have a strong image of the Eiffel Tower, but not be able to place it on map of Paris. One might recall the smell of fish in the Boston Harbor. One might also know various geographical facts, such as Tokyo has roughly 8 million people, London is in the United Kingdom, and Mississippi is spelled with two sets of double S's and one set of double P's. All of these kinds of non-spatial knowledge are included in cognitive collage.

The result of this conceptualization is that geographical information can be displayed in multiple forms, including maps, images, and text. For example, a navigation system can show a map indicating each turn, give a textual description of when and where to turn, or simply show a photograph of where to turn, as you would find with Google Street View. Later, we will see that what is appropriate to show is function of individual preferences and the nature of the space.

Since the publication of Tverksy's (1993) paper, there has been growing empirical evidence to support her conceptualization. Rather than just show a map of an area or route, presenting key images along the route can greatly facilitate recall at the time of travel. In a study conducted in the Netherlands (Oomes, Bojic, and Bazen 2009) found that presenting elderly pedestrians with PDA route maps that are annotated with photographs of landmarks near decision points improved the ability to learn routes. Kaminoyama et al. (2007) found that providing just pictures at intersections, marked with arrows indicating which way to turn, improved performance in terms of both time and errors. The images do not have to be still images, but instead could be video (Chen et al., 2009) or a virtual environment (Meijer, Geudeke, and van den Broek, 2009). Chen et al. (2009) showed improved driver performance if the driver could watch a video of the trip before attempting to navigate on his own. Furthermore, the benefit could be enhance by various graphical techniques, such as slowing the video near a decision point, while panning to toward the corner landmarks, then speeding up in sections between decision points. Meijer et al. (2009) showed that egocentric spatial knowledge of the layout and routes through a virtual supermarket was greatly improved by the use of photorealism. Together, these studies suggest that by minimizing the problem of geolocation (where am I?), one can improve navigation. At the same time, image-based systems take advantage of the strong image memories that are have been well-documented in the cognitive literature (Shepard, 1967; Standing, 1973).

In our own lab, we have been able to implement the notion of a cognitive collage in a library location system for the University of Pittsburgh. Like many colleges, the University of Pittsburgh once had a series of satellite libraries scattered across campus. In a usability study, subjects viewed the locations in the lab and then set out on campus without any wayfinding aids to find the libraries. By having viewed a yoked display of spatial, visual, and verbal information, as shown in Figure 2.4, participants were able to easily locate libraries on campus from memory, whereas before using the system they had little knowledge of the satellite locations (Hirtle and Srinivas, 2010).

Figure 2.4: Library Locator systems for the University of Pittsburgh.

Tversky's (1993) cognitive collage is related to other classifications of spatial knowledge. In particular, the long-standing contention that there are separate propositional and image representations (Rumelhart and Norman, 1985) suggests that knowledge of a spatial layout must be combined with procedural knowledge to move through the space (Crampton, 1992; MacEachren, 1995). There are times when the procedural knowledge may be very efficient and lead to mnemonics. For example, there was once a popular route from Ithaca, NY to Washington, DC began with the following routes: NY-13 to PA-14 to US-15. The easy mnemonic (13-14-15) made the route memorable and required little in the way of survey knowledge or other specific spatial knowledge.

2.3   WAYFINDING

At this point, it is worth looking at what makes directions hard to give and hard to follow. Part of the answer can be found in Carlson et al (2010), which looked at wayfinding in buildings. They focused on three contributing factors as seen in Figure 2.5. These are (1) the spatial structure of the building, (2) the cognitive map that the user constructs for that building, and (3) individual differences in wayfinding skills. The spatial structure can measured using space-syntax tools, as discussed in Section 2.3.2.

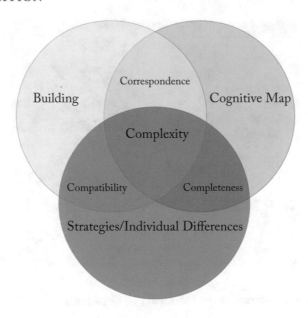

Figure 2.5: Factors that influence the ability to wayfinding in buildings (Carlson et al., 2010).

The most common application of wayfinding would be, in terms of distance, the shortest path or, in terms of travel time, the fastest path, depending on the mode of transportation. The shortest path is the easiest to find given that it depends only on the geometry of network, be it footpaths, roads, or highways, and on your mode of transportation, be it foot, bicycle, car, or truck. An interesting alternative was carried out by Manley, Addison, and Cheng (2015), who analyzed a dataset of 677,411 routes taken by 2,970 minicab drivers in London, UK over a 3-month period. The minicab drivers would be motivated to save time rather than distance, and was achieved through an anchor point strategy of heading to know locations on major routes, while avoiding locations with high "expected" congestion. It is argued that the role of anchors, while not necessarily providing the minimum travel time, will reduce the cognitive load on the driver, as the anchors are is identifiable. In addition, they will lead to interesting asymmetries—what is visible in one direction might not necessarily be visible in the opposite direction. Alizadeh et al (2018) used a similar approach to modeling the selected routes between Montreal and its northern suburb, Laval, which are connected by just nine bridges, which are subjected to a various bottlenecks and delays across the day. The analysis confirmed that using both route-level attributes and anchor points would account for the resulting performance in the network.

Hirtle et al. (2010), in independent research, proposed a naturalistic account for route directions. They examined the posted directions to better understand when parts of directions were tagged as tricky or complicated. The result of their analysis, along with related research (Allen, 2000; Couclelis, 1996; Daniel and Denis, 2004; Klippel et al., 2009; Tenbrink and Winter, 2009; Timpf,

2002) suggests that at a minimum, there are three main problems to address. First, the matching of the environment to a representational system (geolocation) can be a source of difficulty. Second, by its very nature, geographical space varies in complexity. Third, there are expectations that travelers bring to bear in their spatial decisions.

2.3.1   MATCHING PROBLEM

Finding your location on a map is not a trivial exercise. The problem is how to reconcile where you are in a representational system with where you are in geographic space (Davies, Li, and Albrecht, 2010; Davies and Uttal, 2007). This translates into knowing the location on the map (or on the list of directions) and knowing the orientation. Historically, this problem has garnered a large amount of attention, from early studies on map-reading exercises to research on orienteering skills. There are clear individual differences (Crampton, 1992; Montello, 1998) with map-reading skills and perhaps even gender differences (Montello et al., 1999). To use a wayfinding device that tell you to "Turn right in 500 feet" or "Turn right on Main St." one needs to understand where to make a turn in the physical environment. Imagine heading east on Pocusset St, with the goal of turning right on Murray Ave (marked in yellow) in Figure 2.6. There will a fair amount of cognitive overload to make the correct turn. Success will depend on clear instructions and good signage, with perhaps an alert that additional attention in needed to navigate through this intersection. This particular intersection is interesting in that there is additional information, namely elevation, that helps disambiguate two of the choices. Forward Ave is to the right and *down* the hill, while Murray Ave to the right and *up* the hill, which is a feature that no current GPS system would include in their voice directions.

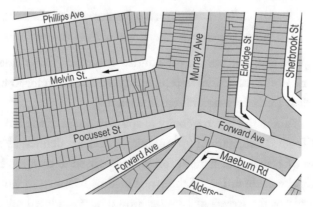

Figure 2.6: A difficult intersection to navigate in Pittsburgh, PA.

Allen (1999) outlined a variety of wayfinding tasks shown in Figure 2.7, which ranged from tasks that occur on a regular basis in familiar space (commute), tasks that occur in unfamiliar spaces for the purpose of learning about the space (explore), and tasks that occur in unfamiliar spaces for the purpose of arriving at a destination (quest). All three tasks involve piloting, but only the activities of explore and quest evoke the cognitive map and, in the case of exploring, also path integration.

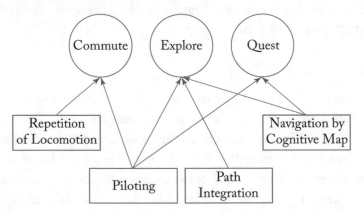

Figure 2.7: Allen's (1999) proposed relations between wayfinding tasks (in circles) and wayfaring means (in rectangles).

2.3.2   HETEROGENEITY OF SPACE

The matching problem can be difficult as natural spaces are noteworthy for their degree of heterogeneity. This arrives, in part, from what has become to known as *Tobler's First Law of Geography* (Miller, 2004), namely:

> *Everything is related to everything else,*
> *but near things are more related than distant things.*

Miller (2004) argues that this almost off-handed comment, first made by Waldo Tobler in 1970, is what leads to the notion of spatial heterogeneity, which can refer to uneven distribution of objects, species or physical forms in a natural environment.

One can also think about the heterogeneity of space in terms of the built environment, which has a slightly different focus. Here, natural (or organic) spaces are defined as those that are created through the interaction of people and natural forces, as opposed to creation by design (Alexander, 1965). Thus, the grid of checkerboard or of the street grid of Manhattan would be planned, while the coastline of California or the streets of London would be considered organic.

In his classic essay, *The City is Not a Tree*, Alexander (1965) made the strong claim that the components of a livable city cannot be partitioned into separate areas, with, say, residential homes in one location and shopping districts in another. Furthermore, recent planned cities that were constructed by a designer to conform to a tree structure, such as Columbia, Maryland, or the Tokyo Bay project by Kenzo Tange, quickly devolve by the intermixing of commercial and residential units. Daycare centers open in the residential sections, while loft apartments appear above businesses.

> "For the human mind, the tree is the easiest vehicle for complex thoughts. But the city is not, cannot and must not be a tree. The city is a receptacle for life. If the receptacle severs the overlap of the strands of life within it, because it is a tree, it will be like a bowl full of razor blades on edge, ready to cut up whatever is entrusted to it. In such a receptacle life will be cut to pieces. If we make cities which are trees, they will cut our life within to pieces" (Alexander, 1965).

The heterogeneity of space also leads to complicated intersections and uneven spacing of roads, which many jurisdictions attempt to regulate, given concerns about traffic safety. The state code of Iowa has gone so far as to discourage the construction of diagonal highways, where diagonal would be assumed to be along an axis that runs either northeast to southwest or northwest to southeast. While this simplifies some intersections, it also leads to many "staircase" paths that require constant turns to stay on the same road, as shown in Figure 2.8.

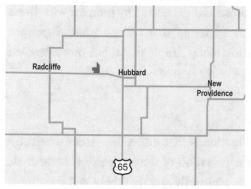

306.9 Diagonal roads—restoring and improving existing roads.

It is the policy of the state of Iowa that relocation of primary highways through cultivated land shall be avoided to the maximum extent possible. When the volume of traffic for which the road is designed or other conditions, including designation as part of the network of commercial and industrial highways, require relocation, *diagonal routes shall be avoided if feasible* and prudent alternatives consistent with efficient movement of traffic exist.

Figure 2.8: Staircase roads in central Iowa and the corresponding regulation.

The most common approach to measuring spatial complexity at present uses the notion of space syntax (Hillier, 2007; Montello, 2007), which is a formal, analytic approach to measuring aspects of the built environment. Space syntax focuses on the connectivity of paths (typically roads in an outside space or hallways in an inside space) and the visibility that the paths provide. For any two locations they are either jointly visible to each other, or there is a minimum number of turns that one could take to become in visual contact. The number turns would then define a conceptual distance between locations. The primary insight of space syntax is that visibility coefficients can be used to measure the overall visibility of the space and the primary axes of travel within the space. Thus, one can use space syntax to quantify the complexity of space in terms of various space syntax measures. Carlson et al. (2010) argued that the intelligibility of the space is a direct predictor of wayfinding difficulty, which is supported by user studies in navigating through large complex buildings, such as hospitals (Haq and Zimring, 2003) and conference centers (Hölscher, Brösamle, and Vrachliotis, 2012).

As a local alternative to address the complexity of space, Klippel (2003) introduced the notion of a wayfinding choremes, which are the primitive conceptual elements of route directions, such as intersections that can be labeled with a generic instruction, such as "head straight," or take a "sharp right." Within this classification, turns are divided in to seven possible actions, each with either a prototypical movement pattern (turn right implies a 90% turn) or an accepted range of action (sharp right implies less than 90%).

Tenbrink and Winter (2009) have extended this approach to examine the granularity of route directions. That is to say, it is well known that human-generated directions vary in granularity with the complexity of the space, where granularity includes both one-dimensional (linear) granularity and two-dimensional (areal) granularity. "Follow State Route 15" would be example where a complex route structure is simplified into a single instruction in terms of one-dimensional granularity, while "Follow the road until you reach the central business district" would be a simplification in terms of two-dimensional granularity. By comparing directions generated by humans with those generated web-based services, Tenbrink and Winter (2009) found that human route directions were much more variable, both in terms of less information along simple paths, but more detailed information at complex decision points.

2.3.3   EXPECTATIONS

The cognitive difficulty in identifying tricky parts of navigation is that difficulties occur when signage and the geometry of the street network violate the expectation of the navigator (Hirtle et al., 2010). There is an expectation that road names will change arbitrarily and that there will be at most one right turn and one left turn at a given intersection. Such expectations build on local knowledge, so that rotaries/roundabouts are not seen as confusing in regions where they are common. In places where cardinal directions are commonly used, head East demands no other instruction. In New Jersey, jug handle intersections, where you turn left from the right lane are not unusual, but in other parts of the U.S. they are rare and, thus, confusing to motorists.

In an interesting test of regional expectations, Davies and Pederson (2001) compared responses from the residents of two grid cities, Eugene (U.S.) and Milton Keynes (UK), on a variety of spatial tasks. The results suggested that regional expectations are strong enough that UK participants failed to take advantage of a urban grid in making directional judgments, whereas U.S. participants, who are more likely to experience grid patterns in cities, used the urban grid to facilitate directional judgments (Davies and Pederson, 2001).

At the same time, roundabouts are common in the UK, but rare in most of the U.S., with the exception of the Northeast. But even in the UK, unusual traffic patterns, such as the Magic Roundabout Magic Roundabout in Swindon, UK which imbeds five mini-roundabouts within a larger roundabout with both an external clockwise (normal) ring and an internal counter-clockwise ring, as shown in Figure 2.9, takes extra caution to navigate.

Figure 2.9: The Magic Roundabout in Swindon, UK.

2.3.4   DEVELOPMENTAL DIFFERENCES

A growing body of literature has documented a wide variety of individual differences in spatial ability that could have a profound influence on the ability to navigate, as well as on the preferred navigational modality. For example, Iaria et al. (2009) found that older adults not only avoid unfamiliar routes and locations, but that they also have more difficulty in creating and accessing cognitive maps of novel environments. In rare cases, some individuals may suffer from a condition known as developmental topographical disorientation (DTD), which was first reported in 2009. This finding has led to new theories of cognitive mapping in terms of the neural bases of spatial cognition in humans and have suggested that wayfinding in complex environments will be impaired for those with DTD (Iaria and Burles, 2016). In related studies, Iaria and his co-workers found an improvement in spatial skills through increased experience of video games that require navigation through a virtual space (Murias et al., 2016). The benefits were seen primarily for navigation and topographical orientation skills when compared with those who did not play video games or played video games that did not require navigation through a virtual space.

CHAPTER 3

Spatial Technologies

Spatial technologies and spatially enable applications grow on almost a daily basis. It is interesting to consider that first personal GPS systems went to market in 1989. After a slow start, aggressive use by manufacturers has resulted in GPS tracking being commonplace in mobile phones, digital cameras, and other portable devices. Peter Morville (2005) is among a group of scholars that has questioned the influx of such devices both from a perspective of usefulness and from issues of privacy. The same device that might be used to make sure an Alzheimer's patient does not wander off from a residential treatment center could be used to monitor the whereabouts of a teenager without their knowledge. Before getting to larger issues, this chapter begins with a look at technologies that communicate spatial knowledge.

The most critical technologies involve some combination of (1) the acquisition of spatial location, (2) a visualization method for describing where you are, and (3) the purpose for completing a spatially relevant task. A prototypical example of such technologies would have initially been the commercially available GPS (found in stand-alone units or mounted in an automobile dashboard). Nowadays, most individuals access GPS through their smartphone and a navigation app. While these kinds of popular navigation systems may first come as mind as meeting these three criteria, there a many other tasks that would also fit this description. The next three sections briefly review methods for gathering and displaying spatial information, which is followed by a discussion of spatially relevant tasks.

3.1   DETERMINING OF SPATIAL LOCATION

To locate a device in an outside environment, GPS uses signals from a minimum of 4 of the 27 satellites in orbit above the earth to calculate the position of the receiver. Like a radio receiver, a GPS only receives signals and does not transmit location information as a matter of course. The initial set of 24 NAVSTAR satellites became fully operational in 1995. The European Union and European Space Agency is in the process of establishing a redundant system called Galileo, that is scheduled to be completed by 2020. Galileo will also provide a significant increase in accuracy and better coverage in northern latitudes.

Current GPS is typically accurate to about 8 m according to http://www.gps.gov. Furthermore, accuracy will degrade in urban environments where tall buildings obscure the direct monitoring of at least four different satellites. However, the situation may be getting better. An early study completed in western Oregon conifer forest with consumer-grade GPS receivers, Wing, Eklund, and Kellog (2005) found that accuracy in forest was in the range of 5–10 m, depending on the amount of growth in the forest. In addition, there are techniques to improve the accuracy of GPS in what are called augmentation systems, which include signals from known locations.

When GPS receivers are not available, there are other options for acquiring locational information. Mobile phones can use triangulation from nearby towers in place of GPS. WiFi units can use the location of the WiFi router to approximate location. In fact, the collection of WiFi routers by location is what got Google in hot water[3] in 2010, as the Street View camera cars were also listening to unencrypted network traffic as part of collecting router information.

Indoor tracking is a more difficult problem. While often referred to as "indoor GPS," the technical solutions are not based on the GPS satellites, but instead require triangulation of other signals, such as wireless routers or a separate set of sensors that are designed for locational information. WiFi location is not based on timing or angular information. Instead, a more common approach is to use the received signal strength from multiple access points to generate a location fingerprint (Kaemarungsi and Krishnamurthy, 2004; Swangmuang and Krishnamurthy, 2008). This can be accomplished several ways, but since received signal strength varies greatly with the architecture and infrastructure, it is better to do a site survey where the received signal strength from multiple access points. This information can then be compared to the profile received by the mobile device to pinpoint the location within the space. At the other end of the spectrum are devices such as RIFD tags that register your presence when you pass through a door to enter a restricted space.

While intelligent devices are useful, it is important to not minimize the usefulness of very unintelligent systems, such as museum digital guides that prompt "When you get to the main hall, press "3" to hear more." While not technologically savvy, such a system relies on the intelligence in the observer and furthermore, if you find yourself engaged in a conversation with your friend, it will not jump in and start talking until you are ready to tell it to speak. Given how many personal technologies interrupt our train of thought, this advantage is not to be minimized.

3.2   DISPLAY OF SPATIAL INFORMATION

3.2.1   CARTOGRAPHIC PRINCIPLES

Cartography as the art and science of map-making provides rich set of principles that can be applied at all levels of geovisualization (Jones, 2010; Longley et al., 2011). While to the novice, cartographic design might appear to be simple, the reality is that both map-making and geographic visualization require the careful balancing of numerous factors. While it is impossible in such a short book to detail all the issues, a few points can direct the reader to the important issues to consider.

---

[3] http://www.nytimes.com/2010/11/11/technology/11google.html

First is the very nature of geographic knowledge, itself. Reginald Golledge (2002) in his presidential address to the Association of American Geographers argued that geographic knowledge as evolved over the past 50 years from declarative knowledge (the cataloging of attributes by spatial location) to cognitive knowledge (associations and inferences about space). Geographic knowledge includes understanding place-to-place relationships and variations, using space on scales from personal to global as pointed out in Section 2.1, and facilitating effective spatial behaviors and activities, be it finding the shortest route, locating the optimal location for new store, evaluating the potential impact of an eminent hurricane, or planning an upcoming holiday trip. The problem of how to communicate not only attributes, but also perceptions, beliefs, emotions, values, and preferences is part of current geographical reasoning. Thus, geographers must consider different elements within a environment, including natural, built, interactional, socio-cultural, and cognitive attributes (Golledge, 2002; Golledge and Stimson, 1997).

The second issue to consider is the question of communication. The ability to extract useful information from map can be view as communication problem where the information is sent through a channel of communication to the intended recipient (Montello, 2002; Poore and Chrisman, 2006; Robinson and Petchenik, 1976; Worboys, 2003). As with Shannon and Weaver's (1949) communication model, there is possibility of information loss between sender and receiver. With geographic knowledge, the information is typically sent from the sender to receiver using spatial display or spatial information system. Montello (2002) argues that map reading is somewhat different from other forms of communication due to preconceived notions about the space or the spatial representation. That is, knowledge that the cartographer was trying to convey might fail to be apprehended by the map reader. At the same time, knowledge that was not intended by the cartographer might be inferred by the reader. Mark Monmonier took the idea of miscommunication seriously in his somewhat tongue-in-cheek book called *How to Lie with Maps* (Monmonier, 1996). In terms of emergency maps, the failure to communicate can have rather severe consequences (Klippel, Freksa, and Winter, 2006).

The third issue to consider are aspects of graphic design, which have been most notably argued by Tufte (1983, 1997), in addition to others (e.g., Kosslyn, 1989; Lloyd, 2000). In particular, maps that require too much superfluous information, such as irrelevant visual information, can lead to difficulty in extracting critical information. Jones (2010) called this *map junk*, which is an extension of *chart junk*, as discussed by (Tufte, 1983), which referred to the extraneous information found in charts and graphs in the popular press. Clean designs that limit the amount of information presented to reader can improve comprehension and help to minimize possible misinterpretations.

The fourth issue relates to the fundamental cartographic principles, especially the properties of scale, generalization, and symbolization. Scale is a fundamental principle of mapping, where a small-scale map presents less detail and greater generalization, while a large-scale map presents greater detail and less generalization, as shown in Figure 3.1. For example, in a large-scale map the details of the exact path of river through a town might be presented, while in a small-scale map only the general curvature can be shown (Worboys and Duckham, 2004). Cadastral maps, which are those used for recording legal boundaries and assessing property taxes, were often drawn to the scale of 1:1,000, which might lead one to think that a large scale, detailed map is necessarily better at presenting information. However, as noted in the insert, the ability to abstract spatial features and generalize over larger areas is requires representations that only smaller scale maps or displays can provide.

"That's another thing we've learned from your Nation," said Mein Herr, "map-making. But we've carried it much further than you. What do you consider the largest map that would be really useful?"

"About six inches to the mile."

"Only six inches!" exclaimed Mein Herr. "We very soon got to six yards to the mile. Then we tried a hundred yards to the mile. And then came the grandest idea of all! We actually made a map of the country, on the scale of a mile to the mile!"

"Have you used it much?" I enquired.

"It has never been spread out, yet," said Mein Herr: "the farmers objected: they said it would cover the whole country, and shut out the sunlight! So we now use the country itself, as its own map, and I assure you it does nearly as well."

Sylvie and Bruno Concluded, [Carroll and Furniss, 1893, p. 168].

Map generalization is the well-known principle that as the scale decreases the amount of detail decreases, including minor curvatures in roads and rivers. On hand-drawn maps. roads will be moved and widen to become more visible, which is one reason that a satellite view could be used as a road map at larger scales (e.g., 1:1,000), but not at smaller scale (e.g., 1:1,000,000). Furthermore, MacEachren (1995) argues that actual map semantics also change with scale. The map symbols (also called map signs) at a large scale would focus on low-level category attributes, such as shops, restaurants, park features, or neighborhood names, while the map signs at a small scale would focus on higher-level category attributes, such as park names, town and city names, or interstate numbers. Thus, there is an interesting conceptual relationship between the spatial scale and the spatial semantics.

Finally, one can extend the discussion beyond traditional maps to the general area of geographic information visualization. There is a growing focus on geovisual analytics, which takes advantage of cognitive and perceptual abilities to process patterns or identify outliers in complex, highly interactive interfaces to geographical information (Fabrikant and Lobben, 2009). This line of research follows from related work on information visualization and has been most notably championed by Natalia and Gennady Andrienko, Sara Fabrikant, Alan MacEachren, Andre Skupin, and the work of the International Cartographic Association (ICA) Commission on Geovisualization (Slocum et al., 2001).

In a related line of research, Klippel (2009) has been examining the perceived similarity of animated plots of a hurricane passing over a peninsula. By comparing empirical data with formal models (e.g., Egenhofer and Al-Taha, 1992; Freksa, 1992), Klippel was able to account for the implied interpretation of animated plots, which are becoming more common to present temporal data.

Map Type	Large Scale	Small Scale
Detail	More Detail	Less Detail
Coverage	Small Area	Large Area
Representative Fraction	1:1,000	1:1,000,000
Ratio	1 m to 1 km	1 m to 1000 km
Generalization	Less Generalization	More Generalization

Figure 3.1: The components of cartographic scale adapted from Jones (2010).

[4] http://www.fig.net/cadastraltemplate/fielddata/d2.htm
[5] http://www.bing.com/maps/

3.2.2   MAPS

Since maps are the primary (but not the only) method of presenting spatial information, it is worth describing in some detail the function of mapping and the mapping process. Davies and Uttal (2007) offer seven properties that maps offer:

a. configurational knowledge that *integrates multiple locations*, which are rarely experienced by movement on the ground;

b. easily perceivable (but not necessarily accurate) information about *distances and directions*;

c. ability to plan *routes* between two distant points;

d. information about invisible, *nonphysical elements* such as town boundaries;

e. the *topology* of the street network;

f. pictorial or iconic *symbolization* of buildings such as schools, bus stops, etc.; and

g. identification *labels* for many individual elements, such as street names or stores.

The first four properties offer inherently spatial information that is difficult to perceive without a map. As pointed out by Davies and Uttal (2007), the standardization of planimetric maps became the common orientation in the 18th century (Elliot, 1987), replacing oblique views, which are easier to comprehend, but necessarily distorted. Current internet mapping provides both street level views in Google Street View and oblique views in Bing maps, in addition to the planimetric views that are either image-based (e.g., satellite view) or map-based (e.g., road maps or shaded relief maps).

It is interesting to note that there has been a return to the 16th century approach. The birds-eye view in Bing maps mimics earlier oblique views without the distortion. An example can be seen in Figure 3.2, which compares Sebastian Münster's 1549 hand-drawn oblique map by with a 2010 computer-generated oblique map of Rome. While looking similar, the projections are quite different in that the computer-generated map is a simple oblique view in which the road network remains identical to the map view, while the historical map is most likely a "cavalier" perspective, in which parallel roads would converge towards a vanishing point. It worth noting that Bing maps label this 40° oblique view as "bird's-eye," in contrast to the traditional bird's-eye view that has been straight down, thus the differences in nomenclature could lead to some confusion.

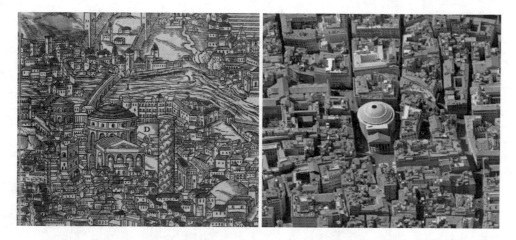

Figure 3.2: Bird's eye views of Rome as hand-drawn[6] in 1549 and as computer-generated using modern day satellite imagery.[7]

3.2.3   SKETCH MAPS

Sketch maps, while often times derided as inaccurate or misleading, have been shown to be a reasonable alternative to cartographic maps or visual images that highlight important details of the space, while downplaying the irrelevant detail (Wang and Schwering, 2009). Kim, Vasardani, and Winter (2016) have developed an automatic approach that extracts spatial objects and their relations from verbal description to produce a plausible sketch map, as seen in Figure 3.3. The approach is inspired by the heuristics that individuals apply in describing place locations. The successful application of the method requires some interesting assumptions about the use of language. For example, a description of the "Sports Center above Campus" would be interpreted as "Sports Center" being north of the campus, while the "Carpark underneath University Square" would be interpreted as the Carpark is located vertically below the University Square. This interesting asymmetry reflect both cultural and linguistical norms.

---

6   http://historic-cities.huji.ac.il/italy/rome/maps/munster_lat_1550_150_b.jpg
7   http://www.bing.com/maps/

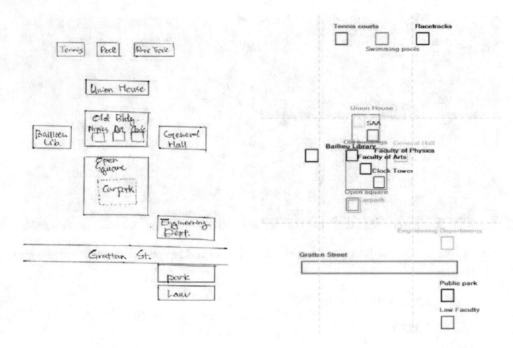

Figure 3.3: Hand-drawn sketch map on the left compared to a computer-generated sketch map on the right (from Kim, Vasardani, and Winter, 2016).

3.2.4 WEB-BASED MAPPING AND VGI

Independent of collecting location information, one often wants to display spatial information in some kind of map like display. Standard interfaces, such as Google Maps, provides a standard user interface that allows for panning and zooming, while the spatial information itself can be stored by the user in KML files. As one simple example, Figure 3.4 shows the local crime data from the University of Pittsburgh from January 2007, each linked the *Pitt News* story about the incident. The design follows the popular mashups that merged data sources into single spatial display, including housingmaps.com, which plots housing posts from Craigslist by city, and the former chicagocrime.org,[8] which plotted crime reports by location and type.

Mashups are rather simple, but more rich interfaces will allow for complex overlays, the inclusion of time lines, or sophisticated 3D interaction with the space. Google Earth (Jones, 2007) and stand-alone GIS applications, such as ArcGIS,[9] provide much greater flexibility, but with the added restriction of downloading specialized software or applications.

---

[8] http://www.holovaty.com/writing/chicagocrime.org-tribute/
[9] http://www.esri.com/

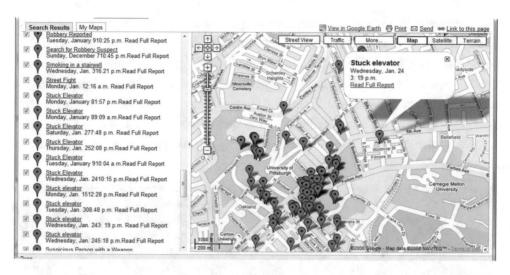

Figure 3.4: Google mashup indicating location of local police incidents.

Of great interest at present are the vast amounts of non-commercial, open data that are being collected. These initiatives, such as Open Street Map,[10] fall under a wider umbrella of *volunteered geographic information* (VGI) (Goodchild, 2007). VGI describes a large number of related activities in which collections of individuals provide geographic information for common consumption, in contrast to relying on the traditional authorities alone to provide maps and spatial information (Goodchild, 2007). This information might be critical in terms of time or just under the radar of in terms of traditional information systems. For example, when the 2010 earthquake hit Haiti, there was little information about the road network or about the damage to the network. As a result, a large group of international volunteers were able to document passable roads, location of temporary shelters and the like, using ground reports, news photographs and satellite imagery, all of which were added to the Open Street Maps of Port-au-Prince and surrounding areas.[11]

An example of VGI comes from the Wikimapia section for Pittsburgh, PA, where the location of food trucks, which appear on daily basis near a college campus to sell food to students, were added by a user. These trucks are part of the informal infrastructure of the campus and would not appear in yellow page directories, service listings, or even traditional Google maps, since they do not reside in permanent buildings with a fixed address. Yet, the information and location of the food trucks is quite useful for students looking for inexpensive meals at lunchtime. Geowikis also provide a platform for the sharing of other kinds of spatial information and further discussed in Section 4.3.

Another aspect of VGI is the recording and display of space-time trails. There are numerous hardware and software combinations that provide this service, including the well-known Nike+

---

[10]   http://www.openstreetmap.org/
[11]   http://blog.okfn.org/2010/01/15/open-street-map-community-responds-to-haiti-crisis/

app that is directed at joggers to record running times and paths. A more generic site, called Every Trail, allows users to upload detailed maps collected on a variety of personal GPS devices, including the iPhone, for display and comment by others.[12] An example of one such map is shown in Figure 3.5. Space-time trails can then be aggregated across individuals to present the joint conception of space by activities as seen Figure 3.6. They might even include anomalies, such as traffic regulations that ignored on a regular basis by motorcycle couriers in London (Turner, 2009). In this case, the resulting "map" does not represent the legal truth, but instead the accepted reality of the collective wisdom.

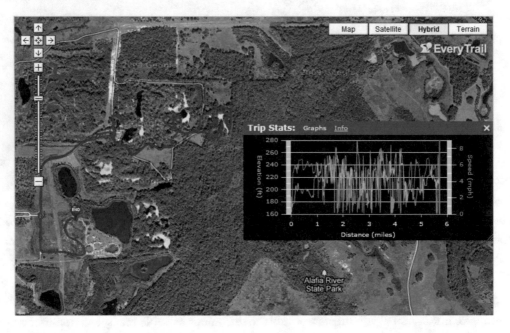

Figure 3.5: **GPS trace from Every Trail** (http://www.everytrail.com/ view_trip.php?trip_id=412832) of a 5.7 mile unicycle trip (trail is marked in red).

---

[12] http://www.nytimes.com/2009/08/20/fashion/20GPS.html

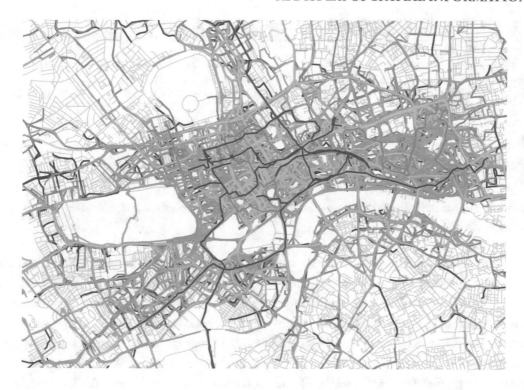

Figure 3.6: GPS traces from motorcycle couriers in central London from Turner (Turner, 2009).

3.2.5   OTHER KINDS OF DISPLAYS

It is also important to realize that there are number of non-geographic spatializations that can highlight the structure behind multivariate spatial data. Here a spatialization is taken to a method of representing non-spatial information in spatial display to highlight non-geographic common-alities (Fabrikant and Skupin, 2005; Skupin and Fabrikant, 2008). In order build it a cognitively plausible information space, it useful to consider the relationship between the semantic properties and the geometric visualization (Fabrikant and Skupin, 2005). This approach leads to numerous options for how to represent properties in a spatial display. Figure 3.7 shows five notions of geo-graphical perspective. For example, a document that changes over time could be represented as trajectory along a path in navigable interface or as a route between two points in a single display (Olsen et al., 1993).

Geographic Perspectives					
Semantic Primitives	Navigable	Vista	Formal	Experiential	Historic
Locus	Landmark	Feature	Occurrence	Object	Point in Time
Trajectory	Path	Route	Relation	Link	Period over Time
Boundary	Edge	Border	Partition	Boundary	Change
Aggregate	District	Region	Set	Container	State

Figure 3.7: Source domains for each possible combination of perspectives and primitives (Fabrikant and Skupin, 2005).

As an example, Figure 3.8: shows a spatializations that was generated by Skupin and Fabrikant (2008). It represents 32 demographic variables using a Kohonen self-organizing map (Kohonen, 1982). The states are each represented by a 32-dimensional vector, where each dimension is a demographic variable. Through an iterative process, each state is located in the space as to minimize the distance between it and its neighbors. The result is a pattern where states with similar demographic profiles (e.g., ND and WY) end up closer together, while states with dissimilar demographic profiles (e.g., DC and MN) end up farther apart. In addition, the individual components planes (6 of which are shown) give insights into the distribution of states. For example, TX, CA, and NM were all strong in Hispanic population as compared with the rest of the states, while UT stood out for having a larger percentage aged 5–17, but lower percentage aged 65+. The post-boomer generation of age 30–39 showed a stronger representation in the states on the left half as compared to states on the right half. Thus, each component plane is free to represent differing patterns depending on the distribution across all 50 states. Skupin and Fabrikant (2008) offered a number of non-traditional visualizations of spatial information, including time-base trajectory plots of indicating divergent and convergent patterns of demographic shifts.

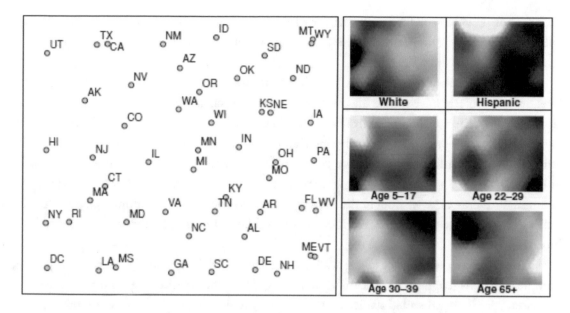

Figure 3.8: Self-organizing map (SOM) representation derived from 32 demographic variables, with the component planes from 6 (out of 32) variables. Higher values are indicated by lighter shading. From Skupin and Fabrikant (2008).

3.3   SPATIALLY RELEVANT TASKS

This chapter has discussed ways of determining one's spatial location and methods of displaying that spatial information. In addition to plotting location, there is often some kind of spatially relevant task that needs to be performed. Depending on the task, different kinds of information would need to be displayed. Simply put, the ice skater on an artificial rank does not care about elevation, while the climber on an artificial climbing wall only cares about elevation. The task determines what information needs to be displayed. This section reviews a few examples of different kinds of spatially relevant tasks that have garnered attention in the literature.

There are a number of specialized projects that have focused on alternative modes of transportation, including cycling, walking, and jogging, each of which has their own constraints. In a related area, there have been several interesting projects looking at how to assist individuals with limited mobility (Loomis et al., 2007; Sobek and Miller, 2006). In this case, there is a need for both specialized interfaces, particularly for blind travelers, as well as specialized routing based on physical constraints. Stairs might be a complete barrier to some, such as wheelchair users, but only a hindrance to others. Likewise, physical stamina can vary. In the end, a system needs to make reasonable tradeoffs that match the user's needs. For example, the U-Access project at the University of Utah that provided intelligent routing for wheelchair users was seen to be useful when students first came to campus and perhaps at the beginning of each term when they are planning routes to new classes (Sobek and Miller, 2006).

It is also a mistake to think that routing is always based on the shortest path or shortest time. Several projects have mined the photo sharing sites, such as Flickr, to create a travel itinerary based on what others visited on their trips (De Choudhury et al., 2010; Popescu and Grefenstette, 2009). This is now possible as photo sharing sites often provide a time and date stamp, along with latitude-longitude information that are automatically collected. Furthermore, users often load a set of photos from a single day or single journey on a single webpage. While one user might have an unusual itinerary, the wisdom of the crowds could lead you to find an optimal plan for the day, such as spending the morning at the local museum followed by a stroll through the old town in the afternoon.

There is also a wide range of applications that can benefit from spatial assistance. As just one example of a non-geographic application, Mary Hegarty, Madeleine Keehner, and their colleagues have been conducting detailed studies on the role of spatial cognition in surgery and related fields (Hegarty et al., 2007, 2009). With the introduction of minimally invasive surgical procedures, such as laparoscopy where a miniature video camera is directed to the surgical location, one loses the haptic cues that existed with more invasive forms of surgery. Keehner and Lowe (2009) showed that haptic cues might be at least informative as visual cues in surgical settings. Thus, it might be incumbent on future interfaces to include a haptic component for the surgeons to respond. In a very different domain, an experimental interface which allows blind sailors to direct a crew on a sailboat has been built using both auditory feedback and a force-feel joystick and has proved successful in tests of the coast of France (Simonnet et al., 2010).

3.4   BEYOND SHORTEST PATHS

Much research in the past has focused on finding the shortest or fastest path, which is a natural variable to minimize when choosing a route. However, there has been an increase in using interesting alternative metrics to optimize the route options. For example, Quercia, Schifanella, and Aiello (2014) used crowdsourced data to quantify whether a location could be considered to be beautiful, quiet, or happy. The routing algorithm created a preferred path that was biased towards those locations with positive attributes, even if it added a few minutes as compared to the shortest path.

It is also worth questioning the amount of detail provided to the navigator. One might think that more detail is more useful, but in fact recent studies suggest that there are benefits to providing less information. Bertel et al. (2017) compared learning new paths with (a) continual access to a map and route directions, as found in most GPS screens or (b) with sparser, tactile device that presented turn information as it was needed. The group in the sparse tactile condition retained greater memory of the route, suggesting that too much information can impede the retention of the spatial information.

CHAPTER 4

Cognitive Interfaces for Wayfinding

There are a number of labs that are working on cognitively driven spatial interfaces and research projects. While it is impossible to list them all, it is worth examining a few of these projects in detail to understand how they differ from generic commercial implementations.

4.1 VARIABLE ROUTING PROGRAMS

When individuals are asked to draw a sketch map, it typically does not follow map conventions. For example, consider the sketch map in Figure 4.1. It differs from a true in map in that many details are left out, while the bridge is shown as a three-dimensional object. In this map, "south" happens to be at the top of the drawing, as that is what made the most sense to the artist, both in terms of the destination and in terms of direction that most would drive to the "The Place," which is across the Birmingham Bridge over the Monongahela River. It is worth noting that the artist almost ran out of room, which is also not uncommon in drawing sketch maps (Freksa, 1999; Tversky, 1999).

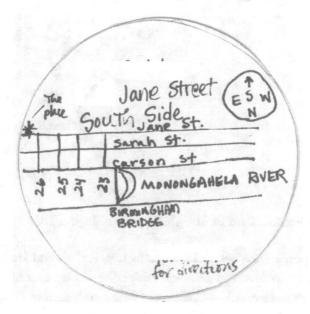

Figure 4.1: Sketch map of a local neighborhood in Pittsburgh.

To mimic human drawn sketch maps, Agarwala and Stolte (2001) created an automatic route drawing program that created a schematic drawing in which the scale was varied so that short segments are exaggerated. The LineDraw algorithm was implemented in commercial system called MapBlast. Since start and end directions are typically shorter segments, this process resulted in more detailed maps at beginning and end of the route, as shown in Figure 4.2, which show the LineDraw directions from the School of Information Sciences at the University of Pittsburgh to the White House in Washington, DC, as rendered at http:mapblast.com. The middle two segments represent distances of 105.1 and 77.9 miles, respectively, while segments on the end are in the range of 0.1–1.0 miles. Obviously, using a fix range would result in little in the way of visible details at the either end of the route, which the reader can easily confirm using any standard routing algorithm. While the LineDraw method itself has not formally tested with human wayfinders, related techniques, discussed below, have been more evaluated through systematic comparisons in the lab (Lee, Forlizzi, and Hudson, 2008).

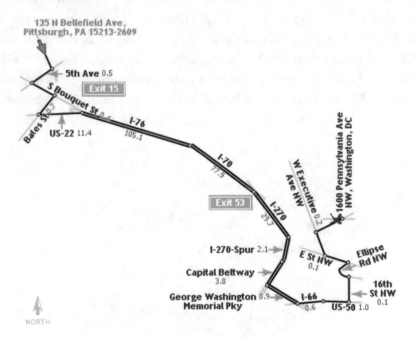

Figure 4.2: Line Draw directions from Pittsburgh, PA to Washington, DC.

The LineDraw approach has been adopted in by Lee, Forlizzi and Hudson (2008) to provide limited visual information to drivers in an in-car navigation display. Part of there is approach is to simplify the space but to present only a small set of landmarks, such as shown in Figure 4.3. (As a small aside, it is remarkable how close their bridge over the river is to the sketch map shown earlier.) The approach is based on presenting a schematic format to the driver where details come into focus as needed.

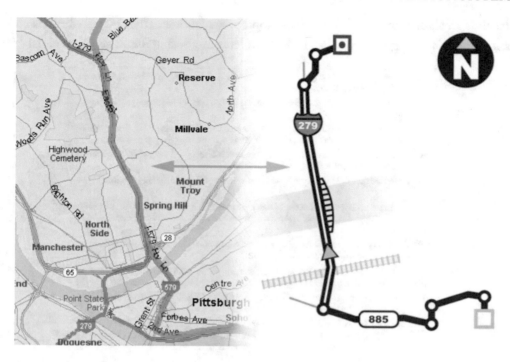

Figure 4.3: Sketch map automatically generated by the MOVE algorithm.

4.2   LANDMARK-BASED WAYFINDING NAVIGATION SYSTEMS

The inclusion of landmarks in directions has been examined in large number of studies over the past decade (Davies and Peebles, 2007; Hirtle, 2007; Michon and Denis, 2001; Raubal and Winter, 2002; Sorrows and Hirtle, 1999; Steck and Mallot, 2000). However, the problem of automatically generating landmarks from open sources has remained a challenge. One possible solution has been proposed by Duckham et al. (2010). In their paper, they generated potential landmarks in Melbourne, Australia by mining a publicly available yellow page service called whereis.com. Whereis generated a large number of potential landmarks that varied in visual and semantic attributes, ranging from notable theaters and hotels to fixed traffic cameras and WiFi hotspots. A new core landmark navigation model (LNM) was developed to order the potential landmarks in terms of their usefulness, which iterated through the possible landmarks near intersection, to determine the strongest possible landmark for inclusion in the directions, as shown in Figure 4.4. Weighting was done by assigning the ratings for the prototypical object in each category. That is, petrol (gas) stations are typically located near a road, prominently marked, well known by name, well lit at night, and so on, while a government consulate, on average, would not share these characteristics.

The result is an algorithm that finds the most appropriate landmark that is located near a corner or along a route, generating directions, such as "Turn left onto Spring Street at the Imperial Hotel."

(i) Generate a route from origin $o \in V$ to destination $d \in V$ from graph $G = (V, E)$ using a standard shortest path algorithm.

(ii) Find the set of POIs $P' \subseteq P$ that lie anywhere along the route (on decision points along the route legs).

(iii) Associate with each POI instance $p \in P'$ the landmark weight, $weight_i(c)$, for the specific user context i and that POI's associated category $c \in C$ such that $category(p) = c$.

(iv) For any POI $p \in P'$ at a decision point, increase the suitability weighting if the POI is on the same side of the road as the upcoming instruction.

(v) Set to zero the weight of every POI, which is not the first instance of its category on each route leg.

(vi) For each decision point, select the POI that is incident with that decision point and has the highest weight. If two or more landmarks have the same weight, arbitrarily select one landmark to use.

(vii) For each route leg that is longer than some travel time threshold t, select the in-leg landmark with the highest landmark suitability.

    (a) If the decision point has no select landmark, generate a new routing instruction of the form "⟨Perform action⟩ onto ⟨Street Name⟩ after ⟨Selected in-leg landmark⟩."

    (b) Otherwise, generate a new routing instruction of the form "Continue ⟨Action⟩ the ⟨Selected landmark⟩" where

        (i) If the selected landmark is point-based, then associated ⟨Action⟩ is "part."

        (ii) Otherwise, if the selected landmark has spatial extents, determine whether the selected landmark abuts or overlaps the route, and set the upcoming ⟨Action⟩ to be "along" (abuts) or "through" (overlaps).

(viii) For each decision point with a selected landmark, generate the routing instruction of the form "⟨Perform action⟩ onto ⟨Street Name⟩ at ⟨Selected landmark⟩."

(ix) For each decision point without a selected landmark and not already preceded by in-leg routing instruction, generate a standard routing instruction of the form "⟨Perform action⟩ onto ⟨Street Name⟩ after ⟨Distance⟩" (Section 4.3.1).

Figure 4.4: Extended LNM Algorithm from Duckham et al. (2010).

4.3   APPLICATIONS THROUGH SOCIAL NETWORKING

The use of spatial information requires both computational and cognitive processes. For example, one can easily calculate the distance from point A to point B along a network of streets to a reasonable degree of accuracy using strict computational measures. Estimating travel times is more difficult but can be done to a fair approximation by including the type of road, traffic flow, time of day, weather conditions and the current traffic load. However, choosing a scenic route or safe cycling path becomes much more difficult. Given the complexity of spatial problem solving and the difficulties in quantifying aesthetic variables, a number of researchers have explored using Web 2.0 technologies as a knowledge source. A few approaches using social networking are listed below.

Cycling routing can be done using an algorithmic method, such as the current Google biking directions. The Google algorithm "tries to put riders on trails and roads with bike lanes or recommended streets as much as possible",[13] which leads to reasonable choices. However, given all the tradeoffs that exist in choosing an optimal biking route, in addition to the need to model bicycle commuting (where you want to minimize time), recreational commuting (where safety and lack of car traffic is a concern), and exercise (where a topographically challenging route might be favored), explicit recommendations might be more useful. Priedhorsky et al. (2007) developed a personalized geowiki that allows individuals to indicate suggested routes and allow users to plan and modify routes based on the a variety of parameters, as shown in Figure 4.5. Other approaches to cycling maps can be found in (Hochmair, 2004; Hochmair and Fu, 2009), as well as the earlier discussion of space-time trails in Section 3.2.

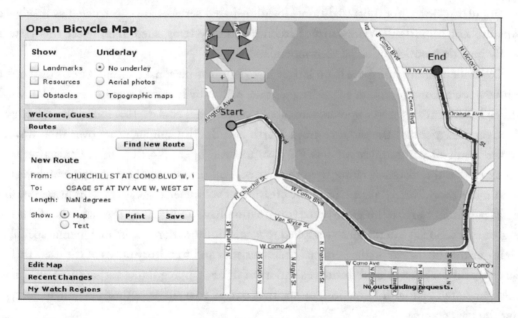

Figure 4.5: Screenshot of a personalized Geowiki for bicycle routing.

Social tagging has been used in an indirect way to understand the conceptualization that individuals have when referencing locations throughout the city. For example, Schlieder and Matyas (2009) analyzed a large collection of over 12,000 photographs of cities posted on Panoramio as a way of understanding how cities are conceptualized by tourists. The works extends the notion of a folksonomy, which are the shared terms that are used to describe a given domain (Gruber, 2008). Schlieder and Matyas (2009) describe the approach as one of collaborative semantics, where the share locations and terminology can be used to describe the structure of city. This not unlike the contrast one finds between the formal structure of city as determined by city planners and engi-

---

[13] http://google-latlong.blogspot.com/2010/05/whats-new-with-biking-directions-on.html

neers, and the common paths of travel that emerge in an analysis of walking patterns using space syntax (Hillier, 1996).

A more direct application of social networking can be found in social navigation services (Bilandzic, Foth, and De Luca, 2008). There is a wide range of services available on the Web from location-based recommender systems to virtual post-it notes and graffiti (Espinoza et al., 2001). As with the previous examples, social navigation services can answer questions that require human judgment, such as the best place to find an inexpensive meal, or what is the best place to get fresh food for a picnic. It is interesting to observe that virtually no one would select a movie based purely on objective facts, such as year, cast, location, and the like, without including some measure of critical or popular reviews. Yet most traditional location-based services are constructed as if subjective notions are not important. Many current recommender systems, such Yelp, reject this view and explicitly include a notion of social recommendation.

The understanding of space is no longer just viewed as personal concept, but instead one can view it as a social construct. Our cognitive maps are driven by how one acquires spatial knowledge, identifies spatial entities, and communicates about space. Uttal et al. (2010) found that Northwestern students exaggerated the distance from North and South Campus more over time was most likely the result of communication acts ("I have to head up to North Campus this afternoon"), which expanded the distance, rather than the physical act of walking the distance, which was only a few minutes away. Recent papers from the creation of volunteered geographic information to use of social networks to share location-based information have emphasized the richness of the social aspects of space. Social interactions as applied to spatial information results in dynamic spatial representations that are based on the personal characteristics and transitory needs of the user. This view reflects a world that can be seen through a variety of filters, tapping into a vast array of information socially generated spatial information, rather than access to a single authoritative map, as typical during the past century.

CHAPTER 5

Open Issues

The book concludes with a discussion of the number of outstanding issues, including concerns about privacy for spatial information, the changing nature of maps as a spatial interface, and a look at the future of user-centered spatial information systems.

5.1 WHAT ARE THE PRIVACY ISSUES WITH REGARD TO SPATIAL INFORMATION?

The inclusion of spatial information raises a number of privacy issues. Some have been documented in rather dramatic fashion, such as in the provocative website called pleaserobme.com that ran for about 6 months in early 2010. The site took public tweets and other social networking posts that might seem innocent, such as "Having pizza at Toni's. Come join in." The problem is not the general call to friends to join in pizza and beer, but rather announcing that your house is empty at this very moment. The extent to which one's Twitter feed is anonymous, this would not be a problem, but if you had earlier posted "I am home having a great breakfast," all with lat/long coordinates, then you are beginning to make too much information available and traceable. Others have argued that such sites are just fear-mongering with little justification to any real danger.[14] Still, it useful to consider how access to your personal locational information might have more serious implications as we move into to new domains of information sharing.

In his book, *Ambient Findability*, Peter Morville (2005) discusses the need for sharing locational information with the need for privacy. In one example, he discussed the Wherify Wireless GPS Personal Locator for Kids, which looks like a watch, but it is literally locked to your child's wrist not unlike the ankle monitors given to those on house arrest. As Morville writes "Are you freaking out yet? Do you find this product disturbing in a profound Orwellian sense? Or, are you on the other side of the fence? Do you see it as yet another miracle of modern convenience? Perhaps you're already on Amazon, placing your order." The ability to track individuals with or without their knowing it is a new area that begs the question that just because we can track movements, does not mean that we should.

Privacy issues hit an emotional nerve in Germany with the introduction of Google Street View in 2010. After much debate, it was decided that individuals would have the right to opt out of having their house or yard shown, as shown in Figure 5.1. Approximately 3% of homes chose this option for a service that began in 2011, which included a company that shared a building with the

---

[14] http://technorati.com/blogging/article/pleaserobmecom-fears-are-totally-unfounded

Google offices in Munich[15]. It was unclear if the request was due to privacy concerns or the irony of having the Google office blurred out.

Figure 5.1: The blurring of house in Germany by Google Street View. [16]

There are often inconsistencies in the how privacy is addressed from country to country. In the U.S., phone books linking names to addresses has been publicly available since 1878. Modern databases have transformed this into cross-linked information that is easily searchable. Michael Goodchild (2006) recently observed the dichotomy between privacy and security when he noted the following.

> We surrender locational privacy whenever we use a credit card, ATM card, or store convenience card, whenever we cross the U.S. border, whenever we drive through an automatic toll barrier, whenever we book an airline ticket, or whenever we turn on our cellphones. These concessions are often made in the interests of convenience. Moreover our own security is arguably strengthened in some circumstances, such as when we call 911 from a cellphone, or when a credit-card company uses locational patterns of purchases in space and time to detect misuse (Goodchild, 2006).

Thus, it may be that giving up some geographical privacy can lead to increased security in other areas. Although, in both cases, the unintelligent use of filters can lead to unintended consequences. There have been numerous cases where a card was cancelled during a European trip because the card owner was not at home to verify the charges. Likewise, while Google Street View tries to blur faces and license plates, it is easy to find examples of over-reach including the blurring

---

[15]   http://news.cnet.com/8301-17852_3-20023292-71.html
[16]   http://google-latlong.blogspot.com/2010/11/street-view-comes-to-20-germancities.html

of politician faces on posters (where they are trying to do everything but hide) and the blurring of small rectangular signs that have the same relative dimensions as license plate, even if not on car, as seen in Figure 5.2.

Figure 5.2: Example of the over blurring of faces and license plate-shaped objects.

Finally, there are several promising empirical approaches to securing privacy of geo-referenced data, such as masking publicly available datasets in ways that do not preclude analytic results. Just as aggregating data by census tracts would preserve privacy, one can develop sophisticate models to mask the actual location of respondents. Kwan and colleagues (Kwan, Casas, and Schmitz, 2004; Kwan and Schuurman, 2004) have shown that by using model appropriate geographical masks, where actual locations are perturbed within the range of an average sized census block in the U.S., privacy protection can be achieved while still able to trace geographically related health patterns.

5.2   IN WHAT WAYS DOES GPS REPLACE THE NEED FOR MAPS ALTOGETHER?

Reference maps have been used for thousands of years both to locate objects and to categorize spaces. They serve as a compact memory device and individuals to locate items, resources and people, as well as communicate to other individuals. By no later than the mid-1800's, maps started to be used for what is now called geovisualization, in addition to the more common purpose of data storage and retrieval. The famous map of the cholera epidemic by English physician John Snow presented convincing visual evidence that the source of cholera outbreak is most likely a single pump in Soho, London (Johnson, 2006). Maps continue to be a useful and fundamental way of representing complex information (MacEachren, 1995). Even non-spatial attributes can benefit from the spatialization of the data for the discovery and representation of patterns and relations (Skupin and Fabrikant, 2008). Clearly, visual displays will continue to be of great importance in the decades to come.

While visual displays have numerous benefits, it is also true that maps can introduce numerous difficulties in many situations. For example, maps are notoriously vague and require interpolation to read accurately (e.g., from the map, the shop appears to be about two-thirds of the way down the road on the right). This is not unlike the classic slide rule, which provide an inexpensive, reliable, all-purpose device for multiplication, which, if read correctly, was accurate to approximately three significant digits. If you need to calculate the area of rectangular space, it was quick and easy, and could be done on the field away from computers and other electronic devices. Unfortunately for slide rules, the emergence of electronic calculators provided an alternative that was just as quick, just as portable, more accurate, and easier to learn. Calculators, which also offered more options, quickly replaced slide rules. The largest American manufacturer of slide rules, Keuffel and Esser, stopped production of slide rules in 1976. It is interesting to note that the final slide rule made by Keuffel and Esser was donated to the Smithsonian Institution, as a cultural relic.[17] Analog devices, in general, have difficulty competing with digital devices, particularly when there is the possibility of human error in reading the analog output.

Not unlike the advent of the calculator, there are numerous geo-applications that bypass the need for maps and, instead, provide spatial information directly to the user or service provider. Consider, for example, the iBurgh app for the iPhone (McNulty, 2009). This application is designed for a single task of reporting a neighborhood problem to the city of Pittsburgh. For example, if you noticed a pothole in your street that has not been filled, you can use the iBurgh app to take a picture of the pothole. The application registers the location and then sends the picture with the geographical coordinates to the city's 311 complaint line. There is no need to describe the location in words or to draw a map of the location to later recall or transmit to the public works department. Spatial information is transmitted directly. In contrast, a similar service to report potholes, fly-tipping, graffiti and the like in the UK[18] does not use smart technology and requires users to enter postal codes, to locate the problem area on a map, and to describe the nature of the problem. All three of these steps can vanish (not unlike the slide-rule) with an intelligent geo-coded application.

Consider direction-giving, which seems like an obvious application that would need a map. Unfortunately, maps suffer from the well-studied alignment problem that requires the observer to locate oneself on both the map and the in the real-world with the appropriate location and orientation (Davies and Peebles, 2007; Levine, 1982). There is also a need to include complex instructions

[17] http://www.comphist.org
[18] http:// www.fixmystreet.com

to get around the "tricky parts" of verbal directions (Hirtle et al., 2010). Furthermore, the cognitive collage principle discussed in Section 2.2.3 suggests that the images of buildings can be just as useful as maps or text in locating oneself in an environment (Tversky, 1993). A distinctive building would be an easy match compared with the task of trying to identify which real-world building corresponds to the red block highlighted on the map (Sorrows and Hirtle, 1999). The influx of image databases, such as Google Street View, allows one to bypass steps and simply match the real-world location to a target image on the mobile device at hand. In fact, we now often find that the 200 × 200 pixel map is becoming the norm for locating information on both websites and mobile screens, as if were just a small gesture to where the object is located.

One should keep in mind that the disappearance of maps is not necessarily an ideal situation. Much has been written on the lack of spatial understanding that is acquired when using guided navigation systems (Ishikawa et al., 2008; Parush et al., 2007). While many math teachers once bemoaned the increased difficulty in explaining logarithms when slide rules were taken out of math and science classes, the lack of spatial awareness seems to be a far greater problem (Downs, 2006; Montello, 2009).

5.3   WHAT IS THE FUTURE OF USER-CENTERED SPATIAL INFORMATION SYSTEMS?

So what does the future hold? Geovisualization and social networking gives us two keys to the future. VGI efforts, such as the Open Street Map initiative in Haiti, are a critical platform for individuals to add knowledge and for other individuals to extract knowledge. Google Earth presents another evolution of maps (Jones, 2007). The interactive abilities of the interface combined with the social networking communities of neo-geographers adding information has led to the ability to view information through a personal filter (Sui, 2008). The evolution of maps leads to personal views that are tailored to personal profiles and goals. In the past, the viewing of maps was seen as such a solitary exercise that researchers would use eye movements to measure the intention of the viewer (Montello, 2002). When maps are instead viewed as a collection of user inputs, then map becomes like the space itself, where individuals can act as both information providers and information consumers. In the end, the information on the map, just like information in the real-world, is a reality that constructed by those who view it.

The use of rich graphics is becoming much more commonplace from complex weather maps in print or in online animations (Hegarty, Canham, and Fabrikant, 2010) or detailed visualizations that are now commonplace in the *New York Times*[19] and in Nate Silver's data intensive blog.[20] As one expands their view beyond maps to include other spatializations, there are a number of excit-

---

[19] http://elections.nytimes.com/2008/results/president/map.html
[20] http://fivethirtyeight.blogs.nytimes.com/

ing Web 2.0 efforts to explore potential visualizations, such as Many Eyes (Segel and Heer, 2010; Viegas et al., 2007), Tableau Public (Zhu and Karmakar, 2010), and GeoTime Stories (Eccles et al., 2007).

In many ways we are at a key point, where for the first time we find the interplay among data rich sources of current statistical information, visualization tools that include both geographic and non-geographic displays, user-interface standards that allow for easy exploration through zoom, pan, filter and search options, and a community of users who are willing to share, annotate, and enrich sources of spatial data. At the same time, the future is not so clear. There is both evidence that geographical information will continue to explode and become as part and parcel of the information milieu and evidence that it will quietly slips behind the scenes to be replaced by spatially intelligent agents. Which reality will emerge is yet to be seen.

CHAPTER 6

For More Information

There are a number of useful sources for anyone wanting to learn more about the theory of spatial cognition and how it applies to geographical design. The best single source would be the recent *Handbook of Behavioral and Cognitive Geography* (2018), edited by Daniel Montello. The chapters cover spatial behavior and decision making, environmental spatial cogntion, cognitive aspects of geographic information, individual and group difference, among other interdisciplinary approaches. Of note is also the variety of disciplines represented by the authors, which include architecture, cartography, cognitive science, computing and information, geography, landscape architecture, linguistics, and psychology. The variety of disciplinary approaches has be fundamental in development of spatial sciences over the past thirty years.

In addition to the recent research in this area, there are several historical sources to consider. On the geographical side, a good place to start would be Alan MacEachren's (1995) comprehensive book on *How Maps Work: Representation, Visualization and Design*, which outlines key elements in the history of cartography. Those without a strong background in geographic information science would also be directed to the third edition of *Geographical Information Systems: Principles, Techniques, Management, and Application* by Longley et al. (2011). Another alternative to consider would be Worboys and Duckham (2004), which is written with strong linkages to research in both cognitive science and user interface design.

On the cognitive side, there is a classic paperback by Rob Kitchin and Mark Blades (2002) on *The Cognition of Geographic Space*, which provides a strong overview. For those interested in wayfinding, there is no better place to start then the comprehensive work edited by Reg Golledge (1999), which reviews literature on human and animal wayfinding, as well as neuroscience and computer models. Another book that looks a wider range of spatial applications would be the edited book by Gary Allen (2007) on *Applied Spatial Cognition*.

Key historical readings would include works by Downs and Stea (1977), Kuipers (1978), and Lynch (1960). On the lighter side, there have also been a few trade books (e.g., Vanderbilt, 2008) in the popular press that address many of the issues discussed. Another thought-provoking book of general scientific interest would be *You Are Here: Why We Can Find Our Way to the Moon, but Get Lost in the Mall* by Colin Ellard (2009), from the University of Waterloo.

Finally, the key conferences in this area would be *GIScience, Spatial Cognition*, and the *Conference on Spatial Information Theory (COSIT)*, while one of most central journals would be *Spatial Cognition and Computation*, published by Taylor-Francis. To measure the impact of the

COSIT series, I conducted an informal analysis[21] of the first four offerings in the COSIT series (1992–1999). I identified 106 different journals or conferences that had cited COSIT papers. These included journals in the fields of Artificial Intelligence, Geographic Information Science, Psychology and Cognitive Science, Geography, Information Science, Linguistics and Language, Philosophy and Logic, Spatial Data and DBMS, Anthropology and Sociology, and User Interfaces and Graphics, indicating a very strong interdisciplinary approach that is present at throughout this conference series.

[21] http://www.geosensor.net/cosit/content/view/19/76/

Bibliography

Agrawala, M. and Stolte, C. (2001). Rendering effective route maps: Improving usability through generalization. In E. Fiume (Ed.), *Siggraph 2001. Proceedings of the 28th Annual Conference on Computer Graphics*. Los Angeles, CA: ACM Press, pp. 241–250. DOI: 10.1145/383259.383286. 39

Alavi, H. S. and Bahrami, F. (2019). Walking in Smart Cities. *Interactions*, 26(2), 66–68. DOI: 10.1145/3301659.

Alexander, C. (1965). The city is not a tree. *Design*, 206, 47–55. 18, 19

Alizadeh, H., Farooq, B., Morency, C., and Saunier, N. (2018). On the role of bridges as anchor points in route choice modeling. *Transportation*, 45(5), 1181–1206. DOI: 10.1007/s11116-017-9761-7. 16

Allen, G. L. (1999). Spatial abilities, cognitive maps, and wayfinding: Bases for individual differences in spatial cognition and behavior. In R. G. Golledge (Ed.), *Wayfinding Behavior: Cognitive Mapping and Other Spatial Processes*. Baltimore, MD: The Johns Hopkins University Press, pp. 46-80. 17, 18

Allen, G. L. (2000). Principles and practices for communicating route knowledge. *Applied Cognitive Psychology*, 14(4), 333–359. DOI: 10.1002/1099-0720(200007/08)14:4<333::AID-ACP655>3.0.CO;2-C. 16

Allen, G. L. (2007). *Applied Spatial Cognition: From Research to Cognitive Technology*. Mahwah, NJ: Lawrence Erlbaum Associates. 51

Andrienko, G. and Andrienko, N. (1999). Interactive maps for visual data exploration. *International Journal of Geographical Information Science*, 13(4), 355–374. DOI: 10.1080/136588199241247. 2

Andrienko, G. and Andrienko, N. (2006). Visual data exploration: Tools, principles, and problems. In P. Fisher (Ed.), *Classics from IJGIS: Twenty Years of the International Journal of Geographical Information Science and Systems*. Boca Raton, FL: CRC Press, pp. 475–479. 2

Bartie, P., Mackaness, W. A., Petrenz, P., and Dickinson, A. (2014). Automated clustering of Landmark Tags in Urban Images. *Proceedings of GISRUK 2014*. Glasgow, UK: Glasgow University. 11

Bertel, S., Dressel, T., Kohlberg, T., and von Jan, V. (2017). Spatial knowledge acquired from pedestrian urban navigation systems. In *Proceedings of the 19th International Conference on Human–Computer Interaction with Mobile Devices and Services (MobileHCI '17)*. New York: ACM. DOI: 10.1145/3098279.3098543. 36

Bilandzic, M., Foth, M., and De Luca, A. (2008). CityFlocks: designing social navigation for urban mobile information systems. Paper presented at the *7th ACM Conference on Designing Interactive Systems*. DOI: 10.1145/1394445.1394464. 44

Carlson, L., Hölscher, C., Shipley, T., and Dalton, R. (2010). Getting lost in buildings. *Current Directions in Psychological Science*, 19(5), 284–289. DOI: 10.1177/0963721410383243. 15, 16, 19

Carroll, L. and Furniss, H. (1893). *Sylvie and Bruno Concluded*. Macmillan. 26

Chalmers, M. (1993). Using a landscape metaphor to represent a corpus of documents. In: Frank A.U., Campari I. (Eds) Spatial Information Theory A Theoretical Basis for GIS. COSIT 1993. *Lecture Notes in Computer Science*, vol 716. Springer, Berlin, Heidelberg. DOI: 10.1007/3-540-57207-4_25. 9

Chang, R., Butkiewicz, T., Ziemkiewicz, C., Wartell, Z., Pollard, N., and Ribarsky, W. (2006). Hierarchical simplification of city models to maintain urban legibility. *SIGGRAPH 2006: ACM SIGGRAPH 2006 Sketches*. DOI: 10.1145/1179849.1180012. 10

Chase, W. (1983). Spatial representations of taxi drivers. In D. Rogers and J. Sloboda (Eds.), *The Acquisition of Symbolic Skills*. New York: Plenum, pp. 391–405. DOI: 10.1007/978-1-4613-3724-9_43. 9

Chen, B., Neubert, B., Ofek, E., Deussen, O., and Cohen, M. F. (2009). Integrated videos and maps for driving directions. *22nd Annual ACM Symposium on User interface Software and Technology*. Victoria, BC, Canada, pp. 223–232. DOI: 10.1145/1622176.1622218. 14

Chen, H., Vasardani , M., and Winter, S. (2017). Geo-referencing place from everyday natural language descriptions. Retrieved from Computing Research Repository (CoRR): http://arxiv.org/abs/1710.03346. 12

Couclelis, H. (1996). Verbal directions for way-finding: Space, cognition, and language. *The Construction of Cognitive Maps*, pp. 133–153. DOI: 10.1007/978-0-585-33485-1_7. 16

Crampton, J. (1992). A cognitive analysis of wayfinding expertise. *Cartographica: The International Journal for Geographic Information and Geovisualization*, 29(3), pp. 46–65. DOI: 10.3138/10TH-4830-2R77-8N21. 15, 17

Cranshaw, J. B., Luther, K., Gage, P., and Sadeh, N. (2014). Curated city: capturing individual city guides through social curation. *CHI '14 Proceedings of the SIGCHI Conference on Human Factors in Computing Systems*. New York: ACM, pp. 3249–3258. DOI: 10.1145/2556288.2557401.

Daniel, M. and Denis, M. (2004). The production of route directions: Investigating conditions that favour conciseness in spatial discourse. *Applied Cognitive Psychology*, 18(1), pp. 57–75. DOI: 10.1002/acp.941. 16

Davies, C., Li, C. L., and Albrecht, J. (2010). Human understanding of space. In M. Haklay (Ed.), *Interacting with Geospatial Technologies*: Wiley Online Library. DOI: 10.1002/9780470689813.ch2. 17

Davies, C. and Pederson, E. (2001). Grid patterns and cultural expectations in urban wayfinding *Spatial Information Theory*. Heidelberg: Springer, pp. 400–414. DOI: 10.1007/3-540-45424-1_27. 20

Davies, C. and Peebles, D. (2007). Strategies for orientation: the role of 3D landmark salience and map alignment. *CogSci 2007: Proceedings of the 29th Annual Conference of the Cognitive Science Society*, pp. 923–928. 41, 48

Davies, C. and Uttal, D. (2007). Map use and the development of spatial cognition. In J. M. Plumert and J. P. Spencer (Eds.), *The Emerging Spatial Mind*. New York: Oxford University Press, pp. 219–247. DOI: 10.1093/acprof:oso/9780195189223.003.0010. 17, 28

De Choudhury, M., Feldman, M., Amer-Yahia, S., Golbandi, N., Lempel, R., and Yu, C. (2010). Automatic construction of travel itineraries using social breadcrumbs. Paper presented at the *Proceedings of the 21st ACM Conference on Hypertext and Hypermedia*, Toronto, Ontario, Canada. DOI: 10.1145/1810617.1810626. 36

Dias, P. and Ramadier, T. (2015). Social trajectory and socio-spatial representation of urban space: The relation between social and cognitive structures. *Journal of Environmental Psychology* 41, December 2014, pp. 135–144. DOI: 10.1016/j.jenvp.2014.12.002. 10

Downs, R. M. (2006). *Learning to Think Spatially: GIS as a Support System in the K-12 Curriculum*. Washington, DC: National Academies Press. 4, 5, 49

Downs, R. M. and Stea, D. (1977). *Maps in Minds: Reflections on Cognitive Mapping*. New York: Harper and Row. 51

Duckham, M. (2015). GI Expertise. *Transactions in GIS*, 19, pp. 399–515. DOI: 10.1111/tgis.12166.

Duckham, M., Winter, S., and Robinson, M. (2010). Including landmarks in routing instructions. *Journal of Location Based Services*, 4(1), pp. 28–52. DOI: 10.1080/17489721003785602. 11, 41, 42

Eccles, R., Kapler, T., Harper, R., and Wright, W. (2007). Stories in geotime. *2007 IEEE Symposium on Visual Analytics Science and Technology*, pp. 19–26. DOI: 10.1109/VAST.2007.4388992. 50

Egenhofer, M. J. and Al-Taha, K. (1992). Reasoning about gradual changes of topological relationships. *Theories and Methods of Spatio-temporal Reasoning in Geographic Space*, pp. 196–219. DOI: 10.1007/3-540-55966-3_12. 27

Egenhofer, M. J. and Mark, D. M. (1995). Naïve geography In A. U. Frank and W. Kuhn (Eds.), *Spatial Information Theory: A Theoretical Basis for GIS*. Berlin: Springer-Verlag, pp. 1–15. DOI: 10.1007/3-540-60392-1_1. 3, 4

Ellard, C. (2009). *You Are Here: Why We Can Find Our Way to the Moon, But Get Lost in the Mall*. New York: Doubleday. 1, 51

Elliot, J. (1987). *The City in Maps: Urban Mapping to 1900*. London: British Library. 28

Espinoza, F., Persson, P., Sandin, A., Nyström, H., E., C., and Bylund, M. (2001). GeoNotes: Social and navigational aspects of location-based information systems. In B. S. Abowd (Ed.), *Ubicomp 2001: Ubiquitous Computing, International Conference*, Atlanta, GA, September 30–October 2. Berlin: Springer, pp. 2–17. DOI: 10.1007/3-540-45427-6_2. 44

Evans, G. and Pezdek, K. (1980). Cognitive mapping: Knowledge of real-world distance and location information. *Journal of Experimental Psychology: Human Learning and Memory*, 6(1), pp. 13–24. DOI: 10.1037//0278-7393.6.1.13. 3, 6

Fabrikant, S. and Lobben, A. (2009). Introduction: Cognitive issues in geographic information visualization. *Cartographica: The International Journal for Geographic Information and Geovisualization*, 44(3), pp. 139–143. DOI: 10.3138/carto.44.3.139. 27

Fabrikant, S. and Skupin, A. (2005). Cognitively plausible information visualization. In J. Dykes, A. M. MacEachren, and M. J. Kraak (Eds.), *Exploring Geovisualization*. Amsterdam: Elsevier, pp. 667–690. DOI: 10.1016/B978-008044531-1/50453-X. 33, 34

Frank, A. U. (1996). The prevalance of objects with sharp boundaries. In P. A. Burrough and A. U. Frank (Eds.), *Geographic Objects with Indeterminate Boundaries*. London: Taylor and Francis, pp. 29–40. 6

Freksa, C. (1992). Using orientation information for qualitative spatial reasoning. In A. U. Frank, I. Campari and U. Formentini (Eds.), *Theories and Methods of Spatio-temporal Reasoning in Geographic Space*. Berlin: Springer, pp. 162–178. DOI: 10.1007/3-540-55966-3_10. 27

Freksa, C. (1999). Spatial aspects of task-specific wayfinding maps. In J. S. Gero and B. Tversky (Eds.), *Visual and Spatial Reasoning in Design*. University of Sydney: Key Centre of Design Computing and Cognition, pp. 15–32. 39

Freundschuh, S. and Egenhofer, M. J. (1997). Human conceptions of spaces: Implications for geographic information systems. *Transactions in GIS*, 2, pp. 361–375. DOI: 10.1111/j.1467-9671.1997.tb00063.x. 5, 6

Friedman, A. and Brown, N. (2000). Reasoning about geography. *Journal of Experimental Psychology: General*, 129, pp. 193–219. DOI: 10.1037/0096-3445.129.2.193. 9

Friedman, A. and Montello, D. R. (2006). Global-scale location and distance estimates: Common representations and strategies in absolute and relative judgments. *Journal of Experimental Psychology: Learning, Memory, and Cognition*, 32, pp. 333–346. DOI: 10.1037/0278-7393.32.3.333. 9

Golledge, R. G. (1999). *Wayfinding Behavior: Cognitive Mapping and Other Spatial Processes*. Baltimor, MD: Johns Hopkins University Press. 51

Golledge, R. G. (2002). The nature of geographic knowledge. *Annals of the Association of American Geographers*, 92(1), pp. 1–14. DOI: 10.1111/1467-8306.00276. 25

Golledge, R. G. and Stimson, R. J. (1997). *Spatial Behavior: A Geographic Perspective*. New York: Guilford Press. 25

Goodchild, M. F. (2006). GIScience ten years after ground truth. *Transactions in GIS*, 10(5), pp. 687–692. DOI: 10.1111/j.1467-9671.2006.01022.x. 46

Goodchild, M. F. (2007). Citizens as sensors: the world of volunteered geography. *GeoJournal*, 69(4), pp. 211–221. DOI: 10.1007/s10708-007-9111-y. 31

Gruber, T. (2008). Ontology of Folksonomy: A mash-up of apples and oranges. *International Journal on Semantic Web and Information Systems*, 3, pp. 1–11. DOI: 10.4018/jswis.2007010101. 43

Haklay, M. (2010). Interacting with Geospatial Technologies. Wiley. DOI: 10.1002/9780470689813. 4

Haq, S. and Zimring, C. (2003). Just down the road a piece. *Environment and Behavior*, 35(1), p. 132. DOI: 10.1177/0013916502238868. 20

Hayes, P. (1979). The naive physics manifesto. *Expert Systems in the Electronic Age*, Edinburgh, Scotland: Edinburgh University Press, pp. 242–270. 3

Hayes, P. (1989). The second naive physics manifesto. In J.R, Hobbs and R. C. Moore (Eds.), Formal Theories of the Commonsense World. Norwood, NJ: Ablex (pp. 1–36). DOI: 10.1016/B978-1-4832-1447-4.50010-9. 3

Hegarty, M., Canham, M., and Fabrikant, S. (2010). Thinking about the weather: How display salience and knowledge affect performance in a graphic inference task. *Learning, Memory,* 36(1), pp. 37–53. DOI: 10.1037/a0017683. 49

Hegarty, M., Keehner, M., Cohen, C., Montello, D., and Lippa, Y. (2007). The role of spatial cognition in medicine: Applications for selecting and training professionals. In G. L. Allen (Ed.), *Applied Spatial Cognition: From Research to Cognitive Technology*. Mahwah, NJ: Erlbaum, pp. 285–315. 36

Hegarty, M., Keehner, M., Khooshabeh, P., and Montello, D. (2009). How spatial abilities enhance, and are enhanced by, dental education. *Learning and Individual Differences*, 19(1), pp. 61–70. DOI: 10.1016/j.lindif.2008.04.006. 36

Hillier, B. (1996). *A Configurational Theory of Architecture*. Cambridge, UK: Cambridge University Press. 44

Hillier, B. (2007). *Space Is the Machine: A Configurational Theory of Architecture*. CreateSpace Independent Publishing Platform. 19

Hirtle, S. C. (1998). The cognitive atlas: Using GIS as a metaphor for memory. In M. J. Egenhofer and R. Golledge (Eds.), *Spatial and Temporal Reasoning in Geographic Information Systems*. Oxford: Oxford University Press, pp. 263–271. 13

Hirtle, S. C. (2007). Landmarks for navigation in humans and robots. In M. E. Jefferies and W.-K. Yeap (Eds.), *Spatial Mapping Approaches in Robotic and Natural Mapping Systems*. New York: Springer. 41

Hirtle, S. C. and Jonides, J. (1985). Evidence of hierarchies in cognitive maps. *Memory and Cognition*, 13, pp. 208–217. DOI: 10.3758/BF03197683. 9

Hirtle, S. C. and Mascolo, M. F. (1991). The heuristics of spatial cognition. *13th Annual Conference of the Cognitive Science Society*. Chicago, IL, pp. 629–634. 4

Hirtle, S. C., Richter, K.-F., Srinivas, S., and Firth, R. (2010). This is the tricky part: When directions become difficult. *Journal of Spatial Information Science*, 1(1). DOI: 10.5311/JOSIS.2010.1.5. 16, 20

Hirtle, S. C. and Srinivas, S. (2010). Enriching spatial knowledge through a multiattribute locational system. In C. Hölscher, T. Shipley, M. Olivetti Belardinelli, J. Bateman, and N. Newcombe (Eds.), *Spatial Cognition VII* (Vol. 6222): Springer Berlin/Heidelberg, pp. 279–288. DOI: 10.1007/978-3-642-14749-4_24. 14, 49

Hochmair, H. H. (2004). Decision support for bicycle route planning in urban environments. In F. Toppen and P. Prastacos (Eds.), *Proceedings of the 7th AGILE Conference on Geographic Information Science*. Heraklion, Greece: Crete University Press, pp. 697–706. 43

Hochmair, H. H. and Fu, J. (2009). Web Based Bicycle Trip Planning for Broward County, Florida. Paper presented at the ESRI User Conference, San Diego, CA. 43

Hölscher, C., Brösamle, M., and Vrachliotis, G. (2012). Challenges in multilevel wayfinding: A case study with the space syntax technique. *Environment and Planning B: Planning and Design*, 39, pp. 63–82. DOI: 10.1068/b34050t. 20

Holyoak, K. and Mah, W. (1982). Cognitive reference points in judgments of symbolic magnitude* 1. *Cognitive Psychology*, 14(3), pp. 328–352. DOI: 10.1016/0010-0285(82)90013-5. 3

Huang, A. C., Ling, B. C., and Ponnekanti, S. (1999). Pervasive computing: What is it good for? Paper presented at the *Proceedings of the ACM International Workshop on Data Engineering for Wireless and Mobile Access*, Seattle, WA. DOI: 10.1145/313300.313414.

Iaria, G. and Burles, F. (2016). Developmental topological disorientation. *Trends in Cognitive Sciences*, 20, pp. 720–721. DOI: 10.1016/j.tics.2016.07.004. 21

Iaria, G., Palermo, L., Committeri, G., and Barton, J. J. (2009). Age differences in the formation and use of cognitive maps. *Behavioral Brain Research*, 196, pp. 187–191. DOI: 10.1016/j.bbr.2008.08.040. 21

Ishikwawa, T. (2016). Spatial thinking in geographic information science: Students' geospatial conceptions, map-based reasoning, and spatial visualization ability. *Annals of the American Association of Geographers*, pp. 76–95. DOI: 10.1080/00045608.2015.1064342. 7

Ishikawa, T., Fujiwara, H., Imai, O., and Okabe, A. (2008). Wayfinding with a GPS-based mobile navigation system: a comparison with maps and direct experience. *Journal of Environmental Psychology*, 28(1), pp. 74–82. DOI: 10.1016/j.jenvp.2007.09.002. 49

Johnson, S. (2006). *The Ghost Map: The Story of London's Most Terrifying Epidemic—and How It Changed Science, Cities, and the Modern World*. New York: Riverhead Books. 48

Jones, C. K. E. (2010). Cartographic theory and principles. In M. Haklay (Ed.), *Interacting with Geospatial Technologies*. Chichester, UK: Wiley, pp. 41–65. DOI: 10.1002/9780470689813. ch3. 24, 25, 27

Jones, M. T. (2007). Google's geospatial organizing principle. *IEEE Xplore*, 27(4), 8–13. DOI: 10.1109/MCG.2007.82. 49

Kaemarungsi, K. and Krishnamurthy, P. (2004). Modeling of indoor positioning systems based on location fingerprinting. *IEEE INFOCOM 2004*. IEEE. DOI: 10.1109/INFCOM.2004.1356988. 24

Kaminoyama, J., Matsuo, T., Hattori, F., Susami, K., Kuwahara, N., and Abe, S. (2007). Walk navigation system using photographs for people with dementia. Human Interface and the Management of Information. Interacting in Information Environments. Human Interface 2007. *Lecture Notes in Computer Science*, vol. 4558. Springer, Berlin/Heidelberg pp. 1039–1049. DOI: 10.1007/978-3-540-73354-6_113. 14

Keehner, M. and Lowe, R. (2009). Seeing with the hands and with the eyes: The contributions of haptic cues to anatomical shape recognition in surgery. In S. Bertel, T. Barkowsky, C. Hölscher, and T. F. Shipley (Eds.), *Cognitive Shape Processing*. Menlo Park, CA: AAAI Press, pp. 8–14. 36

Kim, J., Vasardani, M., and Winter, S. (2016). From descriptions to depictions: A dynamic sketch map drawing strategy. *Spatial Cognition & Computation*, 16(1), pp. 29-53. DOI: 10.1080/13875868.2015.1084509. 29, 30

Kim, J., Vasardani, M., and Winter, S. (2017). Similarity matching for integrating spatial information extracted from place descriptions. *International Journal of Geographical Information Science*, 31(1), pp. 56–80. DOI: 10.1080/13658816.2016.1188930. 12

Kim, M. and Maguire, E. A. (2018). Hippocampus, retrosplenial and parahippocampal cortices encode multicompartment 3D Space in a hierarchical manner. *Cereb Cortex*, 28(5), pp. 1898–1909. DOI: 10.1093/cercor/bhy054. 9

Kitchin, R. and Blades, M. (2002). *The Cognition of Geographic Space*. London: I. B. Tauris. 3, 51

Klippel, A. (2003). Wayfinding choremes. In W. Kuhn, M. F. Worboys, and S. Timpf (Eds.), *Spatial Information Theory: Foundations of Geographic Information Science. Conference on Spatial Information Theory (COSIT)*. Springer, pp. 320–334. DOI: 10.1007/978-3-540-39923-0_20. 20

Klippel, A. (2009). Topologically characterized movement patterns: A cognitive assessment. *Spatial Cognition and Computation*, 9, pp. 233–261. DOI: 10.1080/13875860903039172. 27

Klippel, A., Freksa, C., and Winter, S. (2006). You-are-here maps in emergencies—The danger of getting lost. *Journal of Spatial Science*, 51(1), pp. 117–131. DOI: 10.1080/14498596.2006.9635068. 25

Klippel, A., Hansen, S., Richter, K., and Winter, S. (2009). Urban granularities—a data structure for cognitively ergonomic route directions. *GeoInformatica*, 13(2), pp. 223–247. DOI: 10.1007/s10707-008-0051-6. 16

Klippel, A., Hirtle, S., and Davies, C. (2010). You-are-here maps: Creating spatial awareness through map-like representations. *Spatial Cognition and Computation*, 10(2–3), pp. 83–93. DOI: 10.1080/13875861003770625. 6

Kohonen, T. (1982). Analysis of a simple self-organizing process. *Biological Cybernetics* (Historical Archive), 44(2), p. 135. DOI: 10.1007/BF00317973. 34

Kosslyn, S. M. (1989). Understanding charts and graphs. *Applied Cognitive Psychology*, 3, pp. 185-225. DOI: 10.1002/acp.2350030302. 25

Kuipers, B. (1978). Modeling spatial knowledge. *Cognitive Science*, 2, pp. 129–153. DOI: 10.1207/s15516709cog0202_3. 6, 51

Kuipers, B. (1982). The "map in the head" metaphor. *Environment and Behavior*, 14, pp. 202–220. DOI: 10.1177/0013916584142005. 13

Kwan, M. P., Casas, I., and Schmitz, B. C. (2004). Protection of geoprivacy and accuracy of spatial information: How effective are geographical masks? *Cartographica: The International Journal for Geographic Information and Geovisualization*, 39(2), pp. 15–28. DOI: 10.3138/X204-4223-57MK-8273. 47

Kwan, M. P. and Schuurman, N. (2004). Issues of privacy protection and analysis of public health data. *Cartographica: The International Journal for Geographic Information and Geovisualization*, 39(2), pp. 1–4. DOI: 10.3138/QP47-7743-1162-2675. 47

Lee, J., Forlizzi, J., and Hudson, S. (2008). Iterative design of MOVE: A situationally appropriate vehicle navigation system. *International Journal of Human-Computer Studies*, 66(3), pp. 198–215. DOI: 10.1016/j.ijhcs.2007.01.004. 40

Levine, M. (1982). You-are-here maps. *Environment and Behavior*, 14(2), p. 221. DOI: 10.1177/0013916584142006. 6, 48

Liu, A. S. and Schunn, C. D. (2017). The central questions of spatial cognition. In S. E. Chipman, *The Oxford Handbook of Cognitive Science*. Oxford: Oxford University Press (pp. 169-190). DOI: 10.1093/oxfordhb/9780199842193.013.20. 8

Lloyd, R. (2000). Understanding and learning maps. *Cognitive Mapping: Past, Present, and Future*, London, New York: Routledge, pp. 84–107. DOI: 10.4324/9781315812281-6. 25

Longley, P. A., Goodchild, M. F., Maguire, D. J., and Rhind, D. W. (2011). *Geographical Information Systems: Principles, Techniques, Management, and Applications*, 3rd ed.: John Wiley and Sons. 24, 51

Loomis, J., Golledge, R., Klatzky, R., and Marston, J. (2007). Assisting wayfinding in visually impaired travelers. In G. Allen (Ed.), *Applied Spatial Cognition: From Research to Cognitive Technology*. Mahwah, NJ: Erlbaum, pp. 179–202. 35

Lynch, K. (1960). *The Image of the City*. Cambridge, MA: MIT Press. 13, 51

MacEachren, A. M. (2004). *How Maps Work: Representation, Visualization, and Design*. New York: Guilford Press.

MacEachren, A. M. (1995). *How Maps Work: Representation, Visualization, and Design*. New York: Guilford Press. 6, 15, 26Manley, E. J., Addison, J. D., and Cheng, T. (2015). Shortest path or anchor-based route choice: a large-scale empirical analysis of minicab routing in London. *Journal of Transport Geography*, 43, pp. 123–139. DOI: 10.1016/j.jtrangeo.2015.01.006. 6, 15, 26, 48, 51

Mark, D. M., Freksa, C., Hirtle, S. C., Lloyd, R., and Tversky, B. (1999). Cognitive models of geographical space. *International Journal Of Geographical Information Science*, 13(8), p. 747. DOI: 10.1080/136588199241003. 3

McNamara, T. P., Hardy, J. K., and Hirtle, S. C. (1989). Subjective hierarchies in spatial memory. *Journal Experimental Psychology. Learning, Memory, and Cognition*, 15(2), pp. 211–27. DOI: 10.1037/0278-7393.15.2.211. 9

McNulty, T. (2009). iBurgh lets you complain to city by cell phone. Pittsburgh, PA.: *Pittsburgh Post-Gazette*, August 18, 2009. 48

Meijer, F., Geudeke, B. L., and van den Broek, E. L. (2009). Navigating through virtual environments: Visual realism improves spatial cognition. *CyberPsychology and Behavior*, 12(5), pp. 517–521. DOI: 10.1089/cpb.2009.0053. 14

Michon, P.-E. and Denis, M. (2001). When and why are visual landmarks used in giving directions? In D. R. Montello (Ed.), *Conference on Spatial Information Theory: Foundations of Geographic Information Science*. Berlin: Springer-Verlag. DOI: 10.1007/3-540-45424-1_20. 41

Miller, H. (2004). Tobler's first law and spatial analysis. *Annals of the Association of American Geographers*, 94(2), pp. 284–289. DOI: 10.1111/j.1467-8306.2004.09402005.x. 18

Monmonier, M. (1996). *How to Lie with Maps*. Chicago: University of Chicago Press. DOI: 10.7208/chicago/9780226029009.001.0001. 25

Montello, D. R. (1998). Understanding maps: The viewpoint of cognitive psychology. *Zeitschrift Fur Semiotik*, 20(1–2), p. 91. 17

Montello, D. R. (2002). Cognitive map-design research in the twentieth century: Theoretical and empirical approaches. *Cartography and Geographic Information Science*, 29, pp. 283–304. DOI: 10.1559/152304002782008503. 25, 49

Montello, D. R. (2007). The contribution of space syntax to a comprehensive theory of environmental psychology. In A. S. Kubat, Ö. Ertekin, Y. I. Güney, and E. Eyüboğlu (Eds.), *6th International Space Syntax Symposium Proceedings*. Istanbul, ITÜ Faculty of Architecture. (pp. iv-1–iv-12). 19

Montello, D. R. (2009). Cognitive research in GIScience: Recent achievements and future prospects. *Geography Compass*, 3(5), pp. 1824–1840. DOI: 10.1111/j.1749-8198.2009.00273.x. 49

Montello, D. R. (Ed.). (2018). *Handbook of Behavioral and Cognitive Geography*. Cheltenham, UK: Edward Elgar. DOI: 10.4337/9781784717544. 51

Montello, D. R. and Freundschuh, S. (2005). Cognition of geographic information. In R. B. McMaster and E. L. Usery (Eds.), *A Research Agenda for Geographic Information Science*. Boca Raton, FL: CRC Press, pp. 61–91. DOI: 10.1201/9781420038330.ch3. 3

Montello, D. R., Lovelace, K. L., Golledge, R. G., and Self, C. M. (1999). Sex-related differences and similarities in geographic and environmental spatial abilities. *Annals of The Association of American Geographers*, 89(3), p. 515. DOI: 10.1111/0004-5608.00160. 17

Morville, P. (2005). *Ambient Findability: What We Find Changes Who We Become*. O'Reilly Media. 23, 45

Murias, K., Kwok, K., Castillejo, A. G., Liu, I., and Iraia, G. (2016). The effects of video game use on performance in a virtual navigation task. *Computers in Human Behavior*, 58, pp. 398–406. DOI: 10.1016/j.chb.2016.01.020. 21

Newcombe, N. S. (2018). Three kinds of spatial cognition. In S. L. Thompson-Schill, Stevens' *Handbook of Experimental Psychology and Cognitive Neuroscience: Vol. 3, Language and Thought* (4th ed.). Hoboken, NJ: Wiley, pp. 521–552. DOI: 10.1002/9781119170174.epcn315. 3

Nothegger, C., Winter, S., and Raubal, M. (2004). Selection of salient features for route directions. *Spatial Cognition and Computation*, 4, pp. 113–136. DOI: 10.1207/s15427633scc0402_1. 10, 11

Olsen, K., Korfhage, R., Sochats, K., Spring, M., and Williams, J. (1993). Visualization of a document collection: The VIBE system. *Information Processing and Management*, 29(1), pp. 69–81. DOI: 10.1016/0306-4573(93)90024-8. 33

Oomes, A. H., Bojic, M., and Bazen, G. (2009). Supporting cognitive collage creation for pedestrian navigation. *8th International Conference on Engineering Psychology and Cognitive*

Ergonomics (Vol. LNAI 5639). San Diego, CA: Springer-Verlag. pp. 111–119. DOI: 10.1007/978-3-642-02728-4_12. 14

Parush, A., Ahuvia, S., and Erev, I. (2007). Degradation in spatial knowledge acquisition when using automatic navigation systems. In S. Winter, M. Duckham, L. Kulik and B. Kuipers (Eds.), *COSIT 2007*, Melbourne, Australia (Vol. LNCS, vol. 4736,). Heidelberg: Springer. pp. 238–254. DOI: 10.1007/978-3-540-74788-8_15. 1, 49

Poore, B. and Chrisman, N. (2006). Order from noise: Toward a social theory of geographic information. *Annals of the Association of American Geographers*, 96(3), pp. 508–523. DOI: 10.1111/j.1467-8306.2006.00703.x. 25

Popescu, A. and Grefenstette, G. (2009). Deducing trip related information from flickr. *Proceedings of the 18th International Conference on World Wide Web*. Madrid, Spain: ACM, pp. 1183–1184. DOI: 10.1145/1526709.1526919. 1, 36

Portugali, J. (1996). Inter-representation networks and cognitive maps. In J. Portugali (Ed.), *The Construction of Cognitive Maps*. Dordrecht: Kluwer, pp. 11–43. DOI: 10.1007/978-0-585-33485-1_2. 13

Priedhorsky, R., Jordan, B., and Terveen, L. (2007). How a personalized geowiki can help bicyclists share information more effectively. *Proceedings of the 2007 International Symposium on Wikis*. Montreal, Quebec, Canada: ACM, pp. 93–98. DOI: 10.1145/1296951.1296962. 43

Quercia, D., Schifanella, R., and Aiello, L. M. (2014). The shortest path to happiness: Recommending beautiful, quiet, and happy routes in the city. In *Proceedings of the 25th ACM Conference on Hypertext and Social Media*. ACM, pp. 116–125. DOI: 10.1145/2631775.2631799. 36

Raubal, M. and Winter, S. (2002). Enriching wayfinding instructions with local landmarks. In M. J. Egenhofer and D. M. Mark (Eds.), *Geographic Information Science* (Vol. LNCS 2478). Berlin: Springer-Verlag, pp. 243–259. DOI: 10.1007/3-540-45799-2_17. 41

Richter, K.-F. and Winter, S. (2014). *Landmarks: GIScience for Intelligent Services*. Springer. DOI: 10.1007/978-3-319-05732-3. 12

Robinson, A. H. and Petchenik, B. B. (1976). *The Nature of Maps: Essays Toward Understanding Maps and Mapping*. Chicago: University of Chicago Press. 25

Rumelhart, D. and Norman, D. (1985). Representation of knowledge. In A. M. Aitkenhead and J. M. Slack (Eds.), *Issues in Cognitive Modeling*. Hillsdale, NJ: Erlbaum, pp. 15–62. 15

Schlieder, C. and Matyas, C. (2009). Photographing a city: An analysis of place concepts based on spatial choices. *Spatial Cognition and Computation*, 9, pp. 212–228. DOI: 10.1080/13875860903121848. 43

Segel, E. and Heer, J. (2010). Narrative visualization: Telling stories with data. *IEEE Transactions on Visualization and Computer Graphics*, 16, pp. 1139–1148. DOI: 10.1109/TVCG.2010.179. 50

Shannon, C. and Weaver, W. (1949). *The Mathematical Theory of Information*. Urbana, IL: University of Illinois Press, p. 97.

Shepard, R. N. (1967). Recognition memory for words, sentences, and pictures. *Journal of Verbal Learning and Verbal Behavior*, 6(1), pp. 156–163. DOI: 10.1016/S0022-5371(67)80067-7. 14

Sholl, M. and Nolin, T. (1997). Orientation specificity in representations of place. *Learning, Memory*, 23(6), pp. 1494–1507. DOI: 10.1037/0278-7393.23.6.1494. 6

Simonnet, M., Vieilledent, S., Jacobson, D., and Tisseau, J. (2010). The assessment of non visual maritime cognitive maps of a blind sailor: a case study. *Journal of Maps*, pp. 289–301, 301. DOI: 10.4113/jom.2010.1087. 36

Skupin, A. and Fabrikant, S. (2008). Spatialization. In J. Wilson and S. Fotheringham (Eds.), *The Handbook of Geographical Information Science*: Blackwell Publishing, pp. 61–79. DOI: 10.4135/9781412953962.n194. 33, 34, 35, 48

Slocum, T. A., Blok, C., Jiang, B., Koussoulakou, A., Montello, D. R., Fuhrmann, S., and Hedley, N. R. (2001). Cognitive and usability issues in geovisualization. *Cartography and Geographic Information Science*, 28. DOI: 10.1559/152304001782173998. 27

Sobek, A. and Miller, H. (2006). U-Access: a web-based system for routing pedestrians of differing abilities. *Journal of Geographical Systems*, 8(3), pp. 269–287. DOI: 10.1007/s10109-006-0021-1. 35, 36

Sorrows, M. E. and Hirtle, S. C. (1999). The nature of landmarks for real and electronic spaces. In C. Freksa and D. Mark (Eds.), *Spatial Information Theory*. Berlin: Springer. pp. 37–50. DOI: 10.1007/3-540-48384-5_3. 10, 41, 49

Standing, L. (1973). Learning 10000 pictures. *The Quarterly Journal of Experimental Psychology*, 25(2), pp. 207–222. DOI: 10.1080/14640747308400340. 14

Steck, S. D. and Mallot, H. A. (2000). The role of global and local landmarks in virtual environment navigation. *Presence: Teleoperators and Virtual Environments*, 9, pp. 69–83. DOI: 10.1162/105474600566628. 41

Stevens, A. and Coupe, P. (1978). Distortions in judged spatial relations. *Cognitive Psychology*, 13, pp. 422–437. DOI: 10.1016/0010-0285(78)90006-3. 3

Sui, D. (2008). The wikification of GIS and its consequences: Or Angelina Jolie's new tattoo and the future of GIS. *Computers, Environment and Urban Systems*, 32, pp. 1–5. DOI: 10.1016/j.compenvurbsys.2007.12.001. 49

Swangmuang, N. and Krishnamurthy, P. (2008). Location fingerprint analyses toward efficient indoor positioning. *2008 Sixth Annual IEEE International Conference on Pervasive Computing and Communications (PerCom)*, pp. 100–109. DOI: 10.1109/PERCOM.2008.33. 24

Székely, A. and Kotosz, B. (2018). From fence to wall? Changes in the mental space of border zones in Eastern Europe. *Regional Science Policy and Practice*, pp. 269–282. DOI: 10.1111/rsp3.12120. 8

Tenbrink, T. and Winter, S. (2009). Variable granularity in route directions. *Spatial Cognition and Computation*, 9(1), pp. 64–93. DOI: 10.1080/13875860902718172. 16, 20

Thorndyke, P. and Hayes-Roth, B. (1982). Differences in spatial knowledge acquired from maps and navigation. *Cognitive Psychology*, 14(4), pp. 560–589. DOI: 10.1016/0010-0285(82)90019-6. 3

Timpf, S. (2002). Ontologies of wayfinding: A traveler's perspective. *Networks and Spatial Economics*, 2, pp. 9–33. DOI: 10.1023/A:1014563113112. 16

Tolman, E. C. (1948). Cognitive maps in rats and men. *Psychological Review*, 55, pp. 189–208. DOI: 10.1037/h0061626. 3, 13

Trowbridge, C. C. (1913). On fundamental methods of orientation and imaginary maps. *Science*, 38, pp. 88–897. DOI: 10.1126/science.38.990.888. 3

Tufte, E. R. (1983). *The Visual Display of Quantitative Information (Vol. 16)*, Cheshire, CT: Graphics Press. 25

Tufte, E. R. (1997). *Visual Explanation*. Cheshire, CT: Graphics Press. 25

Turner, A. (2009). The role of angularity in route choice. In K. Hornsby, C. Claramunt, M. Denis, and G. Ligozat (Eds.), *Spatial Information Theory* (Vol. 5756), Springer Berlin/Heidelberg, pp. 489–504. DOI: 10.1007/978-3-642-03832-7_30. 32, 33

Tversky, B. (1981). Distortions in memory for maps. *Cognitive Psychology*, 13(3), pp. 407–433. DOI: 10.1016/0010-0285(81)90016-5. 3

Tversky, B. (1993). Cognitive maps, cognitive collages, and spatial mental models. In A. U. Frank and I. Campari (Eds.), *Spatial Information Theory: Theoretical Basis for GIS*. Berlin: Springer-Verlag. DOI: 10.1007/3-540-57207-4_2. 13, 14, 15, 49

Tversky, B. (1999). What does drawing reveal about thinking. In J. S. Gero and B. Tversky (Eds.), *Visual and Spatial Reasoning in Design*. Sydney, Australia: Key Centre of Design Computing and Cognition, pp. 93–101. 39

Tversky, B. (2000). Levels and structure of cognitive mapping. *Cognitive Mapping: Past, Present and Future*, pp. 24–43. DOI: 10.4324/9781315812281-3. 3

Tversky, B. (2003). Structures of mental spaces: How people think about space. *Environment and Behavior*, 35, 66–80. DOI: 10.1177/0013916502238865. 8

Uttal, D., Friedman, A., Hand, L., and Warren, C. (2010). Learning fine-grained and category information in navigable real-world space. *Memory and Cognition*, 38, pp. 1026–1040. DOI: 10.3758/MC.38.8.1026. 9, 44

Vanderbilt, T. (2008). *Traffic: Why We Drive the Way We Do (and What It Says About Us)*. Knopf. DOI: 10.17077/drivingassessment.1294. 51

Viegas, F., Wattenberg, M., Van Ham, F., Kriss, J., and McKeon, M. (2007). Manyeyes: a site for visualization at internet scale. *IEEE Transactions on Visualization and Computer Graphics*, pp. 1121–1128. DOI: 10.1109/TVCG.2007.70577. 50

Wang, J. and Schwering, A. (2009). The accuracy of sketched spatial relations: How cognitive errors influence sketch representation. In: *Workshop on Presenting Spatial Information: Granularity, Relevance, and Integration at COSIT 2009*. 29

Wing, M., Eklund, A., and Kellogg, L. (2005). Consumer-grade globa positioning system (GPS) accuracy and reliability. *Journal of Forestry*, 103, 169. DOI: 10.1093/jof/103.4.169. 24

Worboys, M. F. (2003). Communicating geographic information in context. In M. Duckham, M. F. Goodchild, and M. F. Worboys (Eds.), *Foundations of Geographic Information Science*. London: Taylor and Francis, pp. 33–45. DOI: 10.1201/9780203009543.ch3. 25

Worboys, M. F. and Duckham, M. (2004). *GIS: A Computing Perspective*, 2nd ed. Boca Raton, FL: CRC Press. DOI: 10.4324/9780203481554. 26, 51

Yeap, W. K. and Hossain, M. (2019). What is a cognitive map? Unravelling its mystery using robots. *Cognitive Processing*, in press. DOI: 10.1007/s10339-018-0895-0. 7

Zhu, Y. and Karmakar, S. (2010). Analysis of a social data visualization web site. *2010 10th International Conference on Intelligent Systems Design and Applications (ISDA)*. Cairo, Egypt: IEEE, pp. 172–175. DOI: 10.1109/ISDA.2010.5687270. 50

Zhu, R. and Karimi, H. A. (2014). Automatic selection of landmarks for navigation guidance article. *Transactions in GIS*, pp. 247–261. DOI: 10.1111/tgis.12095. 11

Author Biography

Dr. Stephen C. Hirtle is a Professor in the School of Computing and Information at the University of Pittsburgh, with joint appointment in the Intelligent Systems Program. He directs the Spatial Information Research Group at the University of Pittsburgh, which conducts research on the structure of cognitive maps, navigation in real and virtual spaces, and computational models for spatial cognition. Dr. Hirtle was the founding co-editor of *Spatial Cognition and Computation* and past-president of the Classification Society of North America. He currently serves as an Associate Editor of the *International Journal Geographical Information Science*. In addition, Dr. Hirtle has had visiting appointments in Geoinformation at the Technical University of Vienna in Austria, Computer Science at Molde College in Norway, the Artificial Intelligence Research Group at the Auckland University of Technology in New Zealand, and Geoinformatics at the University of Augsburg in Germany. He hosted the first North American meeting of International Conference on Spatial Information Theory (COSIT'97), in the Laurel Highlands, outside of Pittsburgh, PA, in October of 1997 and co-chaired the NCGIA Varenius Panel on "Cognitive Models of Dynamic Phenomena and Their Representations" in October of 1998 with Alan MacEachren. He has also served on the Board of the University Consortium for Geographic Information Science.

Printed in the United States
by Baker & Taylor Publisher Services